The Decline of the American Republic

OTHER BOOKS BY JOHN T. FLYNN

The Roosevelt Myth
The Road Ahead: America's Creeping Revo-
   lution
While You Slept: Our Tragedy in America
   and Who Made It
The Lattimore Story

PUBLISHED BY DEVIN-ADAIR

THE
DECLINE
OF THE
AMERICAN
REPUBLIC

And How to Rebuild It

by JOHN T. FLYNN

THE DEVIN-ADAIR COMPANY, *New York,* 1955

CONTENTS

FOREWORD

It is some time since I have felt called on to write a foreword to a book of mine. But it is difficult for me to resist the temptation to provide one for this small volume. As I have watched the course of events in America these last 25 years I have noted with growing apprehension a disturbing phenomenon.

During a century and a half, despite endless differences about policy at any given time, certain principles of organized life were accepted by practically our whole population. These principles involved a collection of moral, social and political concepts. Leaders and groups differed about the means of putting these ideas to work in our society, but there was no important repudiation of the great fundamental concepts themselves.

Then, pressing on the heels of the depression, a new generation was offered a wholly new society—not just a series of reforms of the old. It is fair to say that in its general outlines, and even more in its ultimate development, this new society corresponded with the Fabian philosophy of the British socialists. A vision was conjured before the eyes of our younger citizens of a wholly new and better world—the "Good Society"—that would ensure to all the material essentials of the "good life," along with leisure and a new kind of freedom—freedom from want.

This radiant vision was held up against the dark background of the Great Depression. The promise was benevolent, the hope was bright, and those who doubted it or called attention to its frailties were cast for the role of enemies of the Free World and champions of the wicked world of Wall Street and the Simon Legrees of the big corporations.

It was my lot to tour most of the leading cities of America discussing on the lecture platform these grave problems. Everywhere it was easy to note a growing element in audiences which sought to make me realize that I was defending a dark and ugly world dissolving before the onset of a new and bright dawn of freedom and security for all whose light was just breaking over the Potomac. This baffled me no little, because I had been one of those who had not condoned the evils of certain sections of big business, the banks and Wall Street. I had spent endless hours and acres of pages talking and writing of the disasters that were sure to follow in the wake of the sins of business and politics in those years. The consequences that followed the grave crisis of 1929 were much worse than even I had supposed they would be. I criticized these evils because I believed they were inflicting a serious wound on the free world. But I defended and still defend the system of free enterprise because I believe it to be the only system in which man can live in freedom. But it can survive only if it is managed within the framework of a social order and a government dedicated to preserving it, alert to its defects, and prepared to stimulate its beneficent energies while ensuring freedom to all.

It is difficult to escape the feeling that most of the young men and women who passed through our colleges in the years from 1933 to the present time do not have the faintest conception of the type of government which Americans for a century and a half knew as the American Republic. For this reason I have felt it of the first importance that some effort be made to bring to their attention what I believe to be the greatest disaster of the depression and the wars that followed—the assault upon the American Republic here in America. This assault has progressed so far that, unless arrested now, it will end soon in the complete renunciation of our great constitutional system.

Nothing else engaging the attention of Washington —neither the preservation of the British Empire, nor the salvation of a Europe already drenched in communism, socialism and dictatorship, nor the rescue of an Asia which our government presented on a silver platter to the criminals in the Kremlin—can be permitted to blind the people of America, and particularly our young people, to the project that must be the first and the most challenging of all—the restoration of the American Republic.

Bayside, L. I.,
April, 1955

JOHN T. FLYNN

The Decline of the American Republic

Chapter I

THE

TRAGIC

RETREAT

Whatever the political differences among Americans, there is one point on which all must agree. In this year 1955 we seem to be prosperous, with more people at work at higher wages than at any time in our history. Yet the nation, it must be conceded, is in profound trouble. When we discuss this we usually talk about our difficulties in Asia, the threats of war in Europe, the shadow of Russia over the world, the galling taxes, rising prices, soaring national debt, and widespread corruption in public life, including conduct that borders on treason. But these difficulties do not make up our problem. Neither war, debt, inflation, controls nor corruption are the roots of our greatest concern. They are not *causes*. They are the *effects of an internal social disease*.

Our situation is so grave, the perils that surround us so formidable and our hope of escape without some social convulsion so vague that it is of the first importance that we seek with sober realism the fundamental forces at the base of our trouble.

I lay it down, therefore, as a proposition susceptible of complete proof, that our difficulties do not have their origin in the struggle with Russia or our massive debt and oppressive taxes squandered all over the world. These are the external and visible symptoms of our illness. America is sick. *Our basic disease is that* WE HAVE ABANDONED THE AMERICAN SYSTEM OF GOVERNMENT. We have dismantled the American Republic and reconstructed it on an alien and corrupt plan.

Of course we still speak of our society as the American Republic. But in its essential character it bears only an external and superficial resemblance to the Republic as it existed for 148 years, from 1789 to 1937. Several years ago, Garet Garrett wrote a pamphlet called *The Revolution Was.*[1] I am sure few gave much attention to that brilliant and terrifying document. Now, however, the truth is before our eyes. We have passed through a revolution. World War II and our present embarrassments in Europe and Asia are merely the material manifestations of the basic disease. That disease is nothing less than this: that we have abandoned the fundamental principle on which the American Republic was built. For the perplexities in which we are trapped in Europe, for the confusion and frustration we do not know how to end in Asia, for the crushing debt and taxes at home and the almost unbelievable infusion of treason in our government and our society,

[1] Caxton Printers, Ltd., Caldwell, Idaho, 1944.

there is no remedy so long as we continue *to concern ourselves with the symptoms and ignore the roots of the disease.* We will begin to make some headway against these tragic problems when we have the courage to look with utter realism at the cause and recognize that it will be found not in Europe or Asia but in the crime we have committed against our history, our heritage and our destiny when we began to destroy the American Republic.

These statements, I am sure, will appear fantastic to younger Americans. The man or woman of 40 today was only 14 years old when the stock market collapsed in 1929. They were only 18 when Franklin D. Roosevelt was inaugurated in 1933, amidst the dramatic scenes of disaster which climaxed the depression. It may surprise the reader to be told that *some 46 million voters from 21 to 40 years of age have lived in America under no social conditions save those of depression and war, and under no form of government save that administered by what has been called the New Deal.* It may come as a shock to these people to be told that they have never experienced in their adult years that kind of society which their parents knew as the American Republic, and that they now live in the war-torn, debt-ridden, tax-harried, Red-wracked wreckage of a once imposing edifice of the free society which arose out of the American Revolution on the foundation of the American Constitution.

We have not been dealing with our national social problems intelligently because we have been attacking effects instead of causes. The very first concept we must recapture is this: *That civilized life is not possible without adequate government, but that government itself*

can be the greatest of social evils. The men who framed
the American Constitution were, by a fortunate chance,
familiar with the history of government and tyranny.
They knew that liberty is impossible without government. But they knew also that throughout history *government has been the greatest enemy of liberty.* They
were confronted with the enormous task of erecting a
government for the new nation. They knew that, as of
then, the unsolved problem of society was the erection
of government having all the powers necessary to guard
the peace and the liberties of the people while at the
same time being itself without the means of using those
powers to impair or destroy the people's freedom.

Through long centuries Englishmen in Europe had
been adding one stone upon another to the en-
trenchments of freedom. In Colonial America, deeply
schooled in the traditions of the mother country, our
early statesmen found at last the final elements that
would make the American citizen the freest man who
had ever walked the earth. They used the raw materials
supplied by their ancestors. They did not destroy the
State. They captured it, harnessed it, brought its power
under control and set it to work for free men. But now
we have passed through another revolution in these last
20 years. It can be described as a great and tragic
retreat. We have been rebuilding Big Government—
government too big to be controlled. From this change
flow all the ills and problems from which we now suffer.
We wrestle with the problem of socialist and communist
indoctrination, the wastage of our substance on endless
foreign adventures. But none of these follies is possible
without the thing we call Big Government.

Chapter II

GOVERNMENT

AND

FREEDOM

As this thing—the State—is the monster we have to contend with in these pages, it is important that we understand clearly its essential meaning. We speak of the State or perhaps the government or the nation without defining too sharply these several terms. Randolph Bourne, who had a flare for illuminating such ideas with a gleam of fancy, has written the following revealing paragraph:

"What is the State essentially? The more closely we examine it, the more mystical . . . it becomes. On the Nation we can put our hand as a definite group, with attitudes and qualities exact enough to mean something. On the Government we can put our hand as a certain organization of

7

ruling functions, the machinery of law-making and law-enforcing. The Administration is a recognizable group of political functionaries, temporarily in charge of the government. But the State stands as an idea behind them all, eternal, sanctified, and from it Government and Administration conceive themselves to have the breath of life." [2]

He then offered a practical illustration of this conception. Put a hundred men on an uninhabited island and, by a law of nature, a force springs up among them. They become a little State, even before the hundred men sit around to concert measures of law and personnel. The State is a force inherent in a definable population, which by the laws of existence and the supreme necessity of order, possesses the authority to create for itself a government. The nation is the people. The State is the collective power which inheres in the people. The apparatus of power and compulsion which is set over them to define rights, preserve order and protect the people under whatever authority they agree on is the *government*. The State is the corporate soul of the nation. Government is the apparatus of power employed by the State for its defense and the protection of its citizens. And this apparatus of power is entrusted at any given moment to something called the Administration.

In this group of functions we must never lose sight of the fact that this thing called government is *an apparatus of power*. It is the power to order and control men. It embodies within itself the power to make the rules which regulate the relationships of men, to interpret and enforce those rules and to punish those who

[2] Randolph Bourne, *Untimely Papers*, New York, B. W. Huebsch, 1919, p. 182.

resist them. When this apparatus of power—the government—is delivered into the hands of one man—a monarch—his power to oppress is almost irresistible. And the greater the apparatus of power deposited in his hands the greater will be his capacity to command and enforce obedience. If the total administration of government is deposited in a single person or a single group—an absolute monarch or an aristocracy—it will be able to exploit the people rather than to protect them.

The State, therefore, as the embodiment of authority, is the ultimate source of all tyranny. Even human slavery—the assumed right of one man to own another—is impossible unless it is sanctioned and enforced by the State. It must be clear, therefore, that *the historic struggle of man to be free has consisted in the effort to subdue the State.*

In a republic the ultimate authority is recognized to be in the citizens. But of necessity the people must commit it to agents, depositing all or a part of it with a group of officials who compose the Administration. Once the Administration comes into possession of this apparatus of power, it is essential that the people devise some means of restraining its servants in the use of it. The greatest protection the people can have is the rule by which the Administration is compelled to lay down its powers at stated intervals—surrendering them back into the hands of the people to get a renewal of its authority or effect a transfer to those chosen to succeed it.

But it is at this moment—when the Administration surrenders power back to the people—that society is exposed to its great risk. The authority deposited with the government and wielded by the Administration may be so compulsive and irresistible that the Administration may be able to control the electorate by intimidations and favors. At the moment when the Administration in office must go back to the electorate for a renewal of its commission to govern, a grave danger arises for the people. During the interval in which the electorate is going through the processes of an election, the Administration remains in control. And that control can be used in various ways to influence votes by favors, intimidation or bribery. The power of the Administration may be so great that the electorate will be helpless to escape the formality of renewing its lease of authority. The scattered, divided groups in the constituencies will be no match for the highly organized central Administration and its Janizaries, armed with public funds and with the compulsive machinery of the government.

Chapter III

REPUBLICS

IN

HISTORY

During the last 20 years America has suffered a succession of social and economic dislocations, including a great depression and a great war. We have been so absorbed in these difficulties that we have lost sight of a few simple, elementary principles upon which the free society of America was based. These principles mark the difference between our government and all others in history. And the essential feature of our government, which distinguished it from every other, was the formula we had discovered for *creating a government of great powers but so arranged that while they were adequate to protect us in all our rights they could not be used to exploit or enslave us.*

Our first task, therefore, must be to understand

11

clearly the precise nature of our Republic, which existed in its original form for 148 years. There have been other republics. But we must understand clearly that those other republics of history were utterly different from ours. We may see this readily enough by contrasting ours with other so-called republican governments.

A. ATHENS

Athens is the classic example of the ancient republic. Its authority was deposited in *some* of the people *but not all*. That authority was all embodied in a unitary State—a single governmental apparatus—known as the Republic of Athens. Whoever could get possession of the central republic would have in his, or their hands the total power of government.

There was a citizen body in which reposed the authority of the State. The people were divided into three classes—citizens, metics and slaves. The citizen was one born in Athens of native parents. The metic was a mere inhabitant—one born in another country or born of metic parents. The slave was one captured in war and brought to Athens as a piece of property. Neither metics nor slaves had the right of suffrage. The citizens comprised less than half of the population.

The governing body was the Agora, a legislative institution with no limit upon its powers. It could deprive an Athenian of his citizenship and even reduce him to the condition of a slave. There were no limitations upon the power of a State in which half the population was disfranchised. The Agora was subject utterly to the rule of the majority. But this was in fact far less than the majority of the citizens. The citizen, to vote, had to be present in the Agora in Athens, which, as a practical matter, was not possible to great numbers of citizens who lived at a distance.

There was, indeed, freedom on a scale unknown in any other part of the ancient world—including Rome at a later date. And there was a kind of humane tolerance not common in that age. But we must not forget that Socrates, the first great philosopher of Athens, was compelled to drink the hemlock cup because his teachings ran counter to the prevailing ideas of the society.

B. ROME

Much is made in history and drama of the Roman Republic. But in fact that institution, such as it was, endured for but a brief period. And of course it never came to grips with the dangerous power of the State as the guardian or enemy of freedom. There was for a time a sort of parliamentary mechanism and always there were men in Rome who dreamed of or sought for freedom. During most of its early life Rome was a monarchy. There was a Senate; and a *Comitia* which was purely advisory. After the famous plebeian revolt the kingship was abolished. It was succeeded by a consulate with the *Comitia* as an advisory body *elected by patricians only*. In time the plebs were admitted to certain limited political rights, but only those who owned land were represented. There were grades of citizenship. There were first-class citizens and below them four inferior classes. In any locality they were arranged in five groups—in "centuries." In the top century a few large landowners cast a single vote. In the second century, one vote was shared by a greater number of middle-sized landowners, and so on down to the lowest century where several hundred shared a single vote. Thus the largest landowners exercised a power wholly out of proportion to their numbers. But while the plebs thus gained a foothold in the electorate they were excluded from the administration. Marriage between a plebeian and a patrician was forbidden. Moreover, even this highly diluted share in government was limited to the City of Rome.

In the Italian peninsula outside Rome the people had no votes, though in time they were ceded some limited rights. There was the *Civis Romanus*—citizen of Rome—who owned an estate outside the City and who had to go to the City to exercise his franchise. The *Nomen Latium*—a sort of second-class citizen—had some part in local government but none in the nation, and Rome, as a result of her wars, was filling up with slaves who had no part at all in government. The rudimentary germs of a republic were there. But actually anything moderately resembling a republic appeared only in the last century before Christ, lasted for but a brief space during which time the enemies of freedom came upon the scene to make a mockery of liberty, culminating in that Caesar who brought the turbulent farce to an end.

However, the important fact is that throughout the world and for more than a thousand years after Christ the apparatus of government remained in States possessing unlimited or almost unlimited power, held in the hands of despots. The apparatus of power was vast. Those who chose the administration were a small fraction of the people, and the administration when installed possessed an instrument of authority so great no citizen could cope with it save, perhaps, by violence or revolution.

There were, of course, men who yearned for freedom. But I have been unable to find in these ancient states any general understanding of the principle we are considering here. People hoped only for generous champions. It is a fact of some interest that the Roman State began to sink into the arms of its darkest absolutism more swiftly after the fortunate upper levels of the plebeians had attained the largest measure of freedom in their history.

C. FRANCE

In all these stages of organized society it is important, I repeat, to keep our attention fixed clearly upon the fact that they present a record of governments possessing absolute power and of monarchs, prime ministers and military dictators using this apparatus of power to exploit or oppress society. This is the story of nearly two thousand years of organized societies under the dominion, in varying degrees, of absolute or nearly absolute rulers, relieved here and there by violent and heroic struggles of men to gain small patches of freedom.

In France, up to the time of the Revolution in 1789, the government was absolute, all power residing in a monarch. There were no rights in the citizen save by a grant from the monarch. The French Revolution merely substituted for a brief interval a more frightful and convulsive tyranny until it was liquidated by Napoleon, who made the despotism more intelligent and more efficient and, at least, more orderly. After nearly

2,000 years of history in France, the first attempt at a
free government was the constitution of the Third Republic following the downfall of Napoleon. But a majority of the men who framed that constitution were for
a limited monarchy. They did not, indeed, reestablish
the kingship, but only because they could not agree
upon the king. The Assembly remained in session for five
years before it adopted a constitution. But this consitu-
tion created a government which bore no resemblance
to our own system. The parliament set up was authorized to alter the constitution at will. It defined no constitutional rights of the citizen. It created a Senate and
a Chamber of Deputies to govern, but these two cham-
bers could, by a simple majority, adjourn as a parliament in Paris and move to Versailles, reassemble as a
national assembly and by a simple majority vote completely alter the structure of government. It was the supreme judge of its own rights. Under our form of government *no alteration can be made in the Constitution
save by going back to the source of its power—the people of the sovereign states.*

Under our system, each state is a small republic,
supreme over its internal affairs save where specifically
restrained by the Constitution. The federal government
is a severely restricted government. There is nothing in
France resembling one of our states. There the national
government is supreme. The parliament names the
President and his ministers. It is the depository of all
power, national, provincial and local. The nation is
divided into Departments, Cantons and Communes—
roughly paralleling our states, counties and cities. But
they are completely dominated by the central government. The department—corresponding to our state—is

a mere administrative division. It is headed by a prefect named by the national government. And his every act can be vetoed by the national government. It has a legislature deriving its powers from parliament; its sessions and powers are drastically limited and it can be dissolved at any time by the President of the republic. The mayor of a city is elected by a council, but he is responsible to the prefect of the department. The supreme power is in the national government of the republic, and that power reaches down to the affairs of the smallest village. Once elected, its authority is supreme. The powers it possesses, therefore, are such that they might well be used to oppress the people.

The only protection against this is to be found in a peculiar defect of French politics. There are a large number of parties none of which is able to elect a majority. The party which claims power must depend on a coalition with some other party or, for that matter, with several—often parties of opposite creeds united for the moment on some transient issue. The government of France, however, is such that if a revolutionary party could manage to obtain a solid working majority, the political power in its hands would be so great that it could be used for a swift and drastic alteration in the very nature and structure of the society. There is no effort, as in the United States, to distribute power between the federal government and the provinces—and within the federal government among the executive, legislative and judicial branches with a series of constitutional limitations upon those powers.

D. GREAT BRITAIN

After these commentaries on older or other republics, it is now possible, with Great Britain as an example, to make clear the idea at which we have been aiming. The great problem of men concerned with human freedom throughout the ages was the *conquest of the State*. Nowhere is this made clearer than in the history of England. The State, which had been established to protect men in a society, came to be the instrument used to oppress them. The vast powers of the State deposited in the hands of kings and their ministers were used to exploit society. It is only when we realize this that we can understand the curious cult which came into vogue in the late 18th and middle 19th century generally known as anarchism. It is only when we try to recapture life under those 18th-century monarchies that we can understand how otherwise intelligent men like William Godwin and Pierre Joseph Proudhon could reach the conclusion that government itself was the supreme evil. Godwin held that all evils in society stemmed from the State and its immense mechanisms for repression. After Godwin and Proudhon came writers like Kropotkin and Mikhail Bakunin, the foremost of those philosophers who attributed to the State all the evils of society and who saw no hope for man's redemption from its tyrannies save in anarchy.

Even in the England of 1776 there were men who nursed this fear of the State. There, men had made the greatest advances in the art of social order. The Englishman had, by 1776, come under the protection of Magna Carta and a whole series of established rights, all of which were later embedded in our own Bill of

Rights. But the British subject was very far from having an effective voice in the government of himself. Until the 19th century, Britain's government was a class government, with a monarch and with one branch of the Parliament representing the aristocracy. Gradually, however, in the last 50 years, the power of ultimate representative government was lodged in the people, but with a large measure remaining in the aristocracy.

But all the sovereignty possessed by the people of England is entrusted to one central State. It is in one vast pool of power controlled by one central administration. There are county and local governments, but these are mere agencies of the central government; are created by and can be altered by the central government. The Lords can still interpose delays in action, but the ultimate power is in the Commons as the immediate agency of the people. There is, of course, a great inheritance of fundamental ideas embedded in the affections, the habits and the mores of the people, many defined in statutes and court decisions. These exercise a powerful influence over the conduct of the government. But they are not embedded in a written charter which is free from change save in the manner set out in the charter.

The British constitution is in no wise comparable to the American Constitution. Every right the Englishman has is at the mercy of a mere majority. When, 50 years ago, the socialists set out to alter completely the base of British economic life there was no barrier that stood in the way but a majority of the Parliament. The socialists have since woven over the British people a complexity of laws and controls, backed by authoritarian compulsions, which would startle the Englishman of Edward

VII's day if he could revisit the halls of Westminster. All this has been possible only because of the immense and definitive power of the Commons, subject only to a majority of the electorate.

However, at the time of the American Revolution, the Commons was not the real organ of power. Its members were chosen by an electorate, but no person could vote who did not have a prescribed income and only those towns chartered by the king could send representatives to the Commons. The Tudor kings had created borough constituencies in which the members were named by the king. By 1776 many such boroughs had ceased to exist but were still represented in Parliament, while great cities like Birmingham and Manchester had no representatives in the Commons. In some of these ancient boroughs the bailiffs and a dozen burgesses were the only voters. In Edinburgh and Glasgow there were but a dozen citizens who could vote. There were 75 members of Parliament elected from 35 places literally without inhabitants, 90 from places with less than 50 votes each. These "rotten boroughs" were in fact the property of individual members of the House of Lords, who as patrons designated the members sent to the Commons. In a population of eight million, there were no more than 200,000 persons who could vote for members of Parliament. The monarch was head of the established church and the bishops of that church sat, as they still do, among the Lords.

When our Constitution was adopted, men in every land were ruled by a small fraction of the population grouped around a monarch who held his place by inheritance or conquest and who headed a government which knew no effective restraints save such as proceeded from the good will of a humane ruler or the fears of a timid one. Everywhere the great enemy of man's freedom was government. It is essential to understand clearly that the long struggle of men in the Western world to have an effective part in shaping their own lives has been the struggle against Big Government.

It is of the first importance for the American to grasp the full seriousness of this fact—that the great boon of human freedom has, in the long record of thousands of years, been enjoyed by a mere fraction of the people and for only a brief moment in history. And this great boon attained its furthest advance here on this continent. That advance must be described as the *victory of the people over the dread power of Big Government*.

An institution such as our Republic, of such recent vintage and on only a small patch of the earth, cannot be taken for granted. Particularly is this true when all over Europe we see the limited gains made there disappearing before our eyes. Europe seems to be fatigued by the sacrifices needed to remain free. Even before the final goal is reached, she sinks again behind the dark curtain of government power, her frustrated people forsaking liberty and seeking for security in tyranny.

Chapter IV

THE

AMERICAN

REPUBLIC

Before we can move further into this study, we must have a clear understanding of the device by which the dangerous power of Big Government was solved in the United States. I stress once more the proposition that the young men and women of America under the age of 40 have never, in their adult years, lived under the American Republic in its original form as it existed from 1789 to 1937. Our first care, therefore, must be to recapture for them a realistic picture of our traditional form of government.

I have emphasized the fact that government is an apparatus of power. That apparatus consists of several instruments of power. There is the apparatus of legislation by which the rules for the regulation of the society are made. There is the apparatus of taxation by which the government can reach into every man's pocket for a part of his income. There is the apparatus of justice through which the State imposes on the people the benefit of order and the administration of law. There is the formidable instrument of police power and of military power. *Tyranny may be justly described as the concentration of all these powers in one set of hands— one Administration.* The Administration, be it remembered, is the organized human group of officials who hold and operate the great powers of the State residing in the *Government*.

One great device for guarding the citizens from the powers of the Administration is the suffrage. The ultimate power remains with the citizens. The laws are made and administered and interpreted by officials elected by the people. These officials must return at intervals to the electorate for a renewal of their commissions. When this system was established on a limited scale in England, there is no doubt that the people of England began to enjoy a degree of freedom hitherto unknown. Not only had they established their power to name their officials but they managed, in a long series of struggles against the crown and the nobles, to set up with the force of institutional law a whole series of guarantees generally enumerated in our Bill of Rights.

But this did not go far enough. In England there was but one government—the central government. That government possessed the power of making the laws and policy not merely for the nation as a whole, but for every division and sector, for every community of the nation. In fact the Parliament, with the cabinet, now has in its hands total authority over every sector of British life, subject of course to the right of the electorate to change the personnel of Parliament. In other words, in spite of Britain's long and ever-widening interest in human rights and liberty, the ultimate apparatus of power is centered in one spot—the national Parliament—one huge central apparatus of government, which is insufficient to protect the liberties of the people. Under this arrangement Britain for many generations prospered, grew in wealth and power and in the freedoms of its people. But this system in the end proved inadequate to defend her citizens against a disease that would infect the generation which came along at the turn of this century.

The problem of free government is not achieved by merely committing the enactment and administration of laws to a body of officials elected by the people. *A means must be found of controlling the Administration after it has been elected to power.* Once it is in office, those vast powers of the State are in the possession of the Administration and can be used to purchase or intimidate the electorate. The greater the power it has, the greater will be its ability to control the electorate—buying one group, silencing another. Popular decisions are not made by some mythical coherent force called "the people." The people is made up of good, bad, honest, dishonest, intelligent and ignorant individuals, all with a wide variety of interests. Even the wise and good may be divided by religious, political or economic interests. The people are always split into numerous minorities which nurse a variety of special appetites, prejudices, hopes and opinions. The problem of the politician seeking power is to cultivate the support of these many minorities by promises to satisfy their several and oftimes conflicting hopes. Politicians in a democratic society understand that there is no such thing as a compact majority. Majorities are made up of a number of affiliated minorities—often affiliated only for the moment.

Government is set up to preserve orderly social intercourse and to protect the people. But having set up a government endowed with vast powers which can be abused, *the people must find the means of protecting themselves from that government.*

The obvious device is not to commit all the powers of government into one set of hands, but to divide government into several groupings, each group entrusted with a separate set of functions. In Britain there is one administration—the Parliament to which the executive ministers are responsible. Over the Parliament there is no power save the people as a whole. But in the United States the "division of power" as a principle of government is carried to great lengths. *The government in Washington is not the government of the United States.* It is legally empowered to administer only a very small group of functions.

In America the government consists of a number of republics—49, to be exact. There are the 48 states and the central government. The individual state is a recognized republic endowed with all the authority of government save such faculties as it has deliberately delegated to the central government. Its powers are great, but limited in their territorial extent. The federal republic, on the other hand, is equipped with severely limited powers, but extending over the entire nation. It must never be forgotten that the individual state is a republic and that one of the commitments of the federal government in Article IV, Section 4 of the Constitution is that the "United States shall guarantee to every state in this Union a republican form of government." And this government of the state republic under this Constitution retains in its hands the great mass of political power inherent in the people. To state the principle differently:

1. The federal government has no powers save those specifically granted to it by the states.
2. The individual states have all the powers of government save those specifically denied them by the Constitution.

The states have the powers they exercise by virtue of their own inherent sovereignty. The federal government has no powers except those delegated to it in the Constitution by the states. The whole structure of the federal government is clearly described in the Constitution as being under the authority of the states. The form of government by which the states may rule themselves is not defined—save that it must be a republican government. Every state is ruled by a form of republican government clearly set out in its own constitution and getting its authority from the people of the state itself, and *not* from the federal government.

The federal government is limited in its jurisdiction to only a few areas of administration and legislation. It maintains a national armed service, is supreme in our relations with foreign governments, protects the nation from invasion of the natural rights of citizens enumerated in the Bill of Rights, and it can legislate on matters which are clearly interstate in character. The states, on the other hand, are supreme in all that concerns their internal affairs. The federal government has absolutely no authority to intervene in these.

When we speak of the United States government, we must envision a federal republic operated from Washington and touching the lives and conduct of the people in the states very lightly; and 48 republics exercising all the well-understood functions of government within their own boundaries. In addition to political and social arrangements by law, the state has the authority to provide for its citizens, directly or through its county or municipal governments, whatever services its citizens desire from government and are willing to pay for—through laws governing their personal, family, economic and other relationships, and the services of schools, police, parks, hospitals, playgrounds, fire protection, medical aid, health protection, roads, refuse collection, water systems, etc.

To understand this clearly we have but to look at these two republics—the federal and the state republic —functioning, let us say, in a single state. In 1910 you might have traveled from one end of the state to the other without encountering a single federal official or employee save the postman, or ever feeling the immediate effect of a single federal law. But the government of the state you would meet every hour of the day and night—laws, regulations, services and agents of every description; laws governing business, the roads and streets, and all the relationships of the people of the state with one another; laws governing personal and family relations, property, wills, inheritances, voting rights, election methods and machinery, school buildings, libraries, agricultural schools and stations, police centers, fire houses, hospitals and clinics, courts of law, parks, health protection, recreation centers, charitable institutions, jails, water systems, garbage collections, sewage and drainage—all under the authority of the state directly or through its subdivisions, the counties and municipalities.

Here was all the government a free society needed. Yet, limited as were the powers of the federal government, the leaders in the states, even before the Constitution was adopted by the states, began to fear that these powers exceeded the boundaries of safety. Shortly after the first Congress convened, the first ten amendments were therefore submitted to the states. They defined the boundaries of authority across which neither state nor federal government could step. This was the Bill of Rights. The tenth of this group reads:

"The powers not delegated to the United States by the Constitution, nor prohibited by it to the States, *are reserved to the states respectively, or to the people.*" (Italics added.)

Here was a conscious use of the device I have described for erecting a strong government—strong enough to protect but not strong enough to oppress. I have labored this subject at length because unless this principle is clearly understood it is not possible to understand our Republic or the assaults which have been made on it. The principle, I trust, must now be clear to the reader. The possession of great powers by government is essential to society. However, these powers must be entrusted to officials—known as the Administration. But vast powers in the hands of officials are fraught with danger. They can be used to remain in power and to exploit rather than protect. The only means by which the people can protect themselves is to hold in their hands the right to elect the Administration for a limited period, and force it to return to the people for a renewal of power. But if the powers entrusted to the Administration are very extensive, the Administration can use them to intimidate or buy the electorate and capture a renewal of power.

To be quite certain that this great experiment is clearly understood, let us repeat the description of it in other terms. The apparatus of government was divided into two great sectors. One part of that apparatus of power was confided to the federal government. The remaining part was left in the hands of the states—each state possessing and operating its own government within its boundaries. That part of the engine of power delegated to the federal government was severely limited. That part left with the states was very extensive.

We see at once the striking distinction between this system and the English system. In England all the powers of government are deposited with the national government under king and Parliament. Whatever local machinery is set up gets its existence from the central Parliament. In other words, Parliament, subject to the national electorate, is the supreme sovereign power of the nation. As a matter of necessity it delegates sections of its power to county and local bodies all of whom operate under the supreme authority of the Parliament.

In the United States there are 49 separate and distinct sovereign powers—that is, the 48 states and the federal government. The states are sovereign within their own borders. And the powers exercised by the states are committed to administrations—collections of officials—named by the people of the states. Thus the sovereign powers of the people of the United States are not deposited with a single huge apparatus of government. There are 48 state engines of power each manned by officials chosen in the states. The authority delegated to the central government is lodged in another apparatus of power created and blueprinted by the Constitution and limited severely by that instrument. Then there are a long list of rights inherent in the people and delegated to no one—rights the people have retained in their own hands. But there remained one serious problem. The people who are citizens of the states had to have some agency that would act as a defender of their fundamental rights—those rights embedded in the first ten amendments to the Constitution. They include freedom of speech, press and religion, freedom from unwarranted searches and arrest without warrant, the right to speedy trial, to trial by jury and so forth. The federal government is charged by the Constitution to protect the people in the enjoyment of these great rights as against individuals, state governments and federal officials.

Thus there are 49 separate administrations operating 49 separate and sovereign governmental machines. But the arrangement does not stop there. The federal government, while sovereign, does not have all of its own sovereign authority entrusted to one set of hands. The Constitution sets up the Congress to make the laws. But these laws are administered, not by a parliamentary ministry subject to the Parliament as in England, but by an independent executive getting his power directly from the Constitution. The Congress itself is submitted to a still further restraint. The House of Representatives is named to represent small constituencies within the states, each state having a number of congressmen based on population. But there is the Senate, which represents the sovereign state, each having an equal number of senators. Then, to ensure that neither Senate, House nor Executive oversteps the boundaries of its constitutional powers, there is provided a system of courts, again wholly independent, with power to keep Executive, Senate, House and citizens each severely within the limits of their prescribed powers. Thus the American government is a set of independent governmental machines, operated by separate administrations, with far the greatest portion of governmental power left with the states—each in its own territory—and with still other powers remaining in the hands of the people.

To ensure that the federal government would remain within its narrowly defined boundaries, it was armed originally with only a limited power to tax—that authority of spoliation by which governments exploit and oppress their peoples. The federal government could impose an income tax, but not a graduated tax and, more important, the tax had to be apportioned among the several states, thus greatly limiting its fruitfulness.

Throughout our history the limited role of the federal administration in government was clearly recognized by all parties. And this is evidenced by the manner in which the federal government remained within the circumscribed area. It is further illustrated by the relative costs of federal and state governments, not just in the early days of the Republic, but after 100 years of history. In 1890, the total cost of state and local government in the United States was $1,163,000,000. The total cost of federal government was only $318,000,000. However, most of the money spent by the federal government was on the Army, Navy, veterans' pensions, the postal system and interest on the national debt. For the ordinary civil and economic activities of the nation the federal government spent only $101,800,000 as compared with $1,163,000,000 spent by the state and local governments.

One may insist that this conception of government is no longer applicable to the more highly complex civilization in which we live. This is a point for debate at least. But whether it is or not, there is only one way in which it can be changed. That is by amending the Constitution.

It cannot be said that this conception of the nature of the national government has disappeared through the corrosive processes of time and circumstance. There is no such thing as altering the essential, fundamental principles of our constitutional system by "the corrosive effect of time and circumstance." This can and has happened to the British system on a great scale. This is precisely one of the essential differences between our system and the British. Our Constitution is written and cannot be legally altered either by custom or by changing circumstance or by judicial re-interpretation. It can be done only by going back to the only source of power, and that is to the states and their electorate by constitutional amendment—by means specifically stated in the Constitution.

And, indeed, from 1789 to 1937 no essential change was made (save in the case of the 16th, or Income Tax, Amendment which we shall consider later). The Founders and a long line of political leaders after

them, from Washington, Jefferson, Madison, Marshall
and Hamilton right down to Franklin D. Roosevelt
recognized and affirmed these principles. During the
public debate on the Constitution, James Madison
wrote:

> "*The powers delegated . . . to the federal
> government are few and defined. Those which are
> to remain in the state governments are numerous
> and indefinite.* The former will be exercised prin-
> cipally on external objects, as war, peace, negoti-
> ation, and foreign commerce . . . The powers
> which are reserved to the several states will extend
> to all the objects which, in the ordinary course of
> affairs, concern the lives, liberties, and properties
> of the people, and the internal order, improvement
> and prosperity of the state." (Italics added.)[3]

Madison and his great contemporaries were not
dilettantes in the philosophy of government. They had
studied the writings of the British and French students
of social order. Nearly 30 years before the Constitutional Convention met, the Baron de Montesquieu, the
famous French jurist, had actually outlined his conception of the perfect republic—corresponding precisely to
the model adopted by the men who framed our Constitution. Montesquieu wrote in 1748:

> "This form of government is a convention by
> which several small states agree to become mem-
> bers of a large one, which they intend to form. It
> is a kind of assemblage of societies that constitute
> a new one, capable of increasing by means of new
> associations till they arrive to such a degree of

[3] Federalist No. 45, Modern Library Edition, p. 303.

power as to be able to provide for the security of the united body . . .

"As this government is composed of small republics, it enjoys the internal happiness of each; and with respect to its external situation, it is possessed, by means of the association, of all the advantages of large monarchies." [4]

Alexander Hamilton, the chief exponent of strong government, merely recognized the facts when he said that the definition of a "confederated republic" seems to be "an assemblage of societies or an association of two or more states into one state." [5] In another paper he said the state governments are invested with complete sovereignty. Whole papers by Madison and Jay were devoted to allaying the apprehensions of those who feared a too powerful central government. There was little difference among the men of that day in their conviction that there should be no submergence of the sovereignty of the states in that of the national government.

In 1835—46 years after Washington's inauguration —de Tocqueville, the French student of our young republic, wrote:

"The Constitution of the United States consists of two distinct social structures, connected, and, as it were, encased one within the other; *two governments completely separate and almost independent,* the one fulfilling the ordinary duties,

[4] *Spirit of Laws,* Vol. I, Chap. 1, quoted by Hamilton in Federalist No. 9, Modern Library Edition.
[5] Federalist No. 9, Modern Library Edition.

and responding to the daily and indefinite calls of the community, the other circumscribed within certain limits and only exercising an exceptional authority over the general interests of the country. In short there are *24 small sovereign nations,* whose agglomeration constitutes the body of the Union." (Italics added.)[6]

This idea of government fascinated European students because there was nothing remotely resembling it anywhere in history. In every country, while there were provincial and local governments to administer the laws, these governments derived their powers wholly from a central authority.

There is a notion that our structure of government was changed by our Civil War, which is erroneously supposed to have ended the principle of states' rights. The war settled one question—and one only—namely that the Union was indissoluble. It did not pretend to invade any of the rights of the states. In the platform of 1860 on which Lincoln was elected there appeared this plank:

"The maintenance inviolate of the rights of the states, and especially the right of each state to order and control its own domestic institutions according to its own judgment exclusively, is essential to that balance of power on which the perfection and endurance of our political fabric depends; and we denounce the lawless invasion by armed force of the soil of any state or territory, no matter under what pretext, as among the gravest of crimes."

[6] Alexis de Tocqueville, *Democracy in America,* London, Saunders & Otley, 1838, Vol. I, p. 53.

Lincoln reasserted this great principle in his inaugural address. He said: "I have no purpose directly or indirectly, to interfere with the institution of slavery in the states where it exists. *I believe I have no lawful right to do so.*" Lincoln merely insisted that slavery had no right to move into the territories—not yet states—where it did not exist. During the war Lincoln emancipated the slaves then in durance, but wholly as a war measure. But when the war ended, Republican statesmen correctly concluded something more was needed. Two constitutional amendments—the 13th and 14th—were adopted putting the matter beyond dispute.

Inevitably this question had to be finally resolved and this was done by the Supreme Court in 1873. The Louisiana legislature passed a law controlling the slaughtering of animals. Local butchers claimed that under the 14th Amendment they had privileges that were abrogated by the state law. Justice Miller wrote that it was argued that the 14th Amendment was in some way intended "to fetter and degrade the state governments by subjecting them to the control of Congress, in the exercise of powers heretofore universally conceded to them of the most ordinary and fundamental character." He held the amendment did not alter the relations of state and federal governments save on the matter of slavery. He wrote:

"This Court . . . has always held with a steady and an even hand the balance between state and federal power, and we trust that such may continue to be the history of its relation to that subject so long as it shall have duties to perform which

demand a construction of the Constitution, or of
any of its parts." [7]

It must be remembered that it was the liberals who
insisted on this principle. It was the conservative who
was insistent upon expanding the power of the central
government. As recently as 1944, the late Charles Beard
wrote a lucid and definitive statement of these ideas:

"Powerful as was the structure of the new government . . . it was so formed that, in operation,
checks could be placed on the accumulation of
despotic power in any hands, even in the hands of
the people who had the right to vote in elections.
How to set up a government strong enough to serve
the purposes of the Union and still not too strong
for the maintenance of the liberties of the people?
That was a prime issue in the convention. It had
been in all previous history, and was to be in centuries to come, the central problem in the science
and art of government.

"This question the framers of the Constitution
sought to settle by establishing what is known as
the 'system of checks and balances.' *First of all they
founded each great branch of the government on
a separate basis of political power.* They provided
that members of the House of Representatives
should be elected for a term of two years by persons entitled to vote under certain laws of the respective states; that the senators should be elected
for terms of six years by the legislatures of the
states; and that the President should be elected for
four years by electors chosen as the state legisla-

[7] Slaughter House Cases, 16 Wall. 36 (1873).

tures might decide . . . Members of the federal judiciary were to be selected by the President and the senate, both one degree removed from direct popular vote . . .

". . . under the methods provided for the choice of representatives, senators, President and federal judges, no political party or faction could get possession of the whole government at a single election. In the long run, through a period of years, the persistent will of the popular majority might prevail. Yet at no moment could the 'snap judgment' of a popular majority prevail in all departments of the federal government.

"Moreover, within the very structure of the government, power was so distributed that no branch could seize all of it, unless the others deliberately abdicated." (Italics added.)[8]

To complete this thesis, there should have been little left to question when the man who was later to defy this settled principle gave his testimony on the subject. On July 16, 1929, Franklin D. Roosevelt, then governor of New York, addressing a conference of governors, said:

"Our nation has been a successful experiment in democratic government, because the individual states have waived in only a few instances their sovereign rights . . . *But there is a tendency, and to my mind a dangerous tendency, on the part of our national government, to encroach, on one excuse or another, more and more upon state supremacy.* The elastic theory of interstate commerce,

[8] Charles A. and Mary R. Beard, *Basic History of the United States,* Garden City, 1944, pp. 131, 132.

for instance, has been stretched almost to the breaking point to cover certain regulatory powers de-
sired by Washington.[9] (Italics added.)

On another occasion in a radio address, March 2,
1930, when he was an avowed candidate for the presidency, Mr. Roosevelt said:

> "As a matter of fact and law, the governing
> rights of the states are all of those which have not
> been surrendered to the national government by
> the Constitution or its amendments. Wisely or un-
> wisely, people know that under the 18th Amend-
> ment Congress has been given the right to legis-
> late on this particular subject [liquor], but this is
> not the case in the matter of a great number of
> other vital problems of government, *such as the
> conduct of public utilities, of banks, of insurance,
> of business, of agriculture, of education, of social
> welfare and of a dozen other important features.
> In these, Washington must not be encouraged to
> interfere.*
>
> "The proper relations between the government
> of the United States and the governments of the
> separate states thereof depend entirely, in their
> legal aspects, on *what powers have been volun-
> tarily ceded to the central government by the states
> themselves.*" (Italics added.)

Then he added:

> "The preservation of this 'Home Rule' by the
> states is not a cry of jealous Commonwealths seek-

[9] *Public Papers and Addresses of Franklin D. Roosevelt,* New York,
Random House, 1938, Vol. I, p. 367.

ing their own aggrandizement at the expense of sister states. It is a fundamental necessity if we are to remain a truly united country. The whole success of our democracy has not been that it is a democracy wherein the will of a bare majority of the total inhabitants is imposed upon the minority, but that it has been a democracy where through a division of government into units called the states the rights and interests of the minority have been respected and have always been given a voice in the control of our affairs. This is the principle on which the little state of Rhode Island is given just as large a voice in our national Senate as the great state of New York." [10]

Thus this principle stood recognized and championed by Mr. Roosevelt 141 years after it was first enunciated by the framers of the Constitution.

If, in the presence of new and modern conditions, this system was no longer suited to our 20th Century society, the way of altering the Constitution is laid down in that instrument—namely by constitutional amendment. This, of course, is difficult, but it is not impossible. The Constitution has been subjected to 22 amendments. It is a fact of the profoundest significance, however, that in every case but two, the amendments were designed to *restrict still further the power of the federal government*. One exception was the Income Tax Amendment. The other was the Prohibition Amendment which gave the federal government jurisdiction over the subject of liquor, and this was repealed 13 years after its passage.

Our system of government is based upon certain

[10] *Ibid.*, pp. 569, 570.

great fundamental principles which transcend in importance the year-to-year policies of administration. At the bottom of it all is the recognition of the age-old fact that government itself is one of the dangers most to be feared, and that while society must have government, society must also be protected from its powers. Our political leaders from Washington to Franklin D. Roosevelt have given complete acquiescence to this principle. And as late as 1935, Chief Justice Hughes— an advocate of strong government—said in a famous decision:

> "The Constitution established a national government with powers deemed to be adequate, as they have proved to be both in war and peace, but these powers of the national government are limited by the constitutional grants . . . 'The powers not delegated to the United States by the Constitution nor prohibited by it to the states, are reserved to the states respectively, or to the people.'" [11]

To complete the significance of the decision in the case from which these sentences are taken—the famous Sick Chicken case of the NRA—the decision was unanimous, concurred in by Justices Brandeis, Cardozo and Holmes, the three most eminent liberals on the bench at the time.

Let us now see if we can recapture a faithful picture of the great American system—the culminating chapter in man's war against the enemy of freedom, the all-powerful State. In a remote period, power in England was deposited in a monarch. In time an aristocracy shared it with the crown and, after endless struggles,

[11] A. L. A. Schechter Corp. v. U.S., 295 U.S. (1935).

that power was deposited with the king, nobles and Commons. Little by little the king's authority would vanish and the aristocracy would be reduced to a severely limited share. Finally the franchise would be extended to all the people. But the total power of the central State would be immense. The central government of Britain can do anything for which it can get a majority in the Commons and a vote of the majority of the people. This is not true of America. The vast powers of government are deposited in the hands of 48 separate states and one central republic. In each of these states, the Administration is split into three sectors— legislative, executive and judicial—all operating on specifically blueprinted powers, and all chosen by separate electorates. In short the vast and dangerous apparatus of power—the government—is split up into a large number of separate parts, each entrusted to a separate administration and subjected to many enumerated limitations.

Only in America was this solution reached. There were, indeed, other federal governments. The German empire, the Italian monarchy, the French government— all these were nations formed out of a federation of smaller kingdoms, dukedoms or principalities. But they were in no sense a federation of separate republics. When brought together into a monarchy or empire or even a republic (as in the case of France) their individual identity was wholly submerged in the central State into which they were combined. They presented a spectacle in no way resembling our own assemblage of individual republics which derived their existence and their authority not from the central republic but from their own inherent sovereignty. That sovereign entity we call the State, namely that total of sovereign power which was deposited in the central government and the separate local governments, lost the power to oppress. Since its complete authority was in the hands of neither king, lords nor Commons, this new State was a dismantled one. Parts of the functions of government were abolished, and what remained derived its authority from a variety of constituencies. This carefully guarded government had all the power necessary to protect the people, without having enough to oppress and exploit them. All the essential energies of governmental power were around, but could be used by no one class or faction. This was the American Republic—an association of small republics, each retaining its power over its own people, while surrendering to a central republic only such powers as were essential to the liberties and rights of all as defined in a written charter.

This was the supreme work of the ages in the sphere of human government; the crowning effort of man to make the State his servant rather than his master. I do not contend that this great work was all done in America. Leaders had preached and died on the block through centuries. The long struggle had been going on in England and later in America for over a thousand years. The first settlers to land upon these shores brought with them an accumulation of principles and institutions of free government. Placed happily in a favorable environment, their descendants completed the task—or nearly so. They reared finally the American Republic, which has provided for its citizens the greatest degree of security and well-being with the greatest degree of freedom ever known in this world.

Chapter V

THE

GREAT

DEPRESSION

The American Republic we have described existed for 144 years. In the 22 years since 1933 it has been subjected to a profound change, accomplished without any change in the actual words of the Constitution. It has been done by a sheer usurpation of power by the federal government. This could not, of course, have been brought about without certain favoring circumstances. The chief influence was what has come to be known as the Great Depression of 1929.

Our system is geared to be a society for free men. It is not a machine that can be operated by pulling levers from a central control tower. It is composed of moving parts—human beings—each operating on its own power and with its own steering gear. It cannot be supposed that this vast nation of free men will move mechanically around a common orbit without encountering occasional interruptions. The socialist supposes that this immense aggregation of human beings can be made to function with the highest efficiency if all men will surrender themselves to the direction of an all-wise and all-powerful central State ordered and steered by the all-wise and benevolent men who control it.

The causes of depressions in a free society are not far to seek. This economic society is a collection of producing and distributing operations involving raw materials moving from mines and farms and from across seas through a multitudinous succession of processes into the shops of merchants and thence to the homes of consumers. All these agencies are directed by free men. All mixed up in this complex succession of activities at every turn are investors, workers, producers, merchants and consumers endowed with differing tastes and abilities, and with freedom of choice. Does any rational mind suppose that such a system will move around in a smooth orbit, without occasional jerks and interruptions arising from the frailties of men and the limitations of machines? There is another force called Progress, continuously discarding old materials and processes for new and more dynamic ones.

The inevitable consequence of these influences must be an occasional slowing down here and there. These pauses will be ordinarily local in area—little depressions here and there, confined to some industry or locality. It may happen at certain times that these individual depressions will assault some larger area of the economic system, when the resulting inertia will be far more serious. And it can also happen that at longer intervals a concurrence of individual and local depressions, arising out of the greed or folly or just plain ignorance of enterprisers may spread its evil effects over a whole nation.

Of course we must recognize that the chief causes of serious depressions are booms, which are created by enormous and unhealthy expansion of credit, particularly bank credit. The depression is the headache after the spree. The depression of 1929 was due to several causes which ordinarily would have forced business into a moderate decline. But the extraordinary energy of the boom of 1923 to 1929 was created chiefly by a wild orgy of speculation of every sort, superimposed on a group of more or less normal activities—and ending in a disorderly crash. Here are the factors which were responsible for the boom:

(1) Making up the grave shortages in peacetime goods after World War I. (2) A building boom on credit following the cessation of building during the war. (3) The automobile boom—new models following each other in dizzy succession and sold on credit. (4) Wide and epochal changes in our habits, brought about by the automobile, such as immense road building on bond issues, and new communities in the suburbs along with the building of community necessities—all on mortgage money. (5) The erection of some 26,000 moving picture theatres on credit, to accommodate the rising movie industry. (6) With this went a wild expansion of installment credit on everything—autos, furniture, new radio sets, even clothes. (7) Devastated Europe added to the orgy through buying here of all sorts of raw materials, mostly on credit.

There were two other very serious sources of the

boom. One was a wild witches' dance of security speculation on credit. The other was the unhealthy development of new and dangerous experiments in banking,
largely through what was called "holding company"
and "affiliate" banking. The ownership of almost every
kind of industry was being converted into stocks and
bonds, listed on exchanges and distributed in bold selling drives to millions of new and uninformed investors
and speculators. A theory got around that we were in a
New Era—some sort of new-fangled world of endless
plenty, no longer subject to the laws of arithmetic and
gravity. It had its philosophers and prophets just as did
the New Deal which succeeded it. Farmers, clerks,
school teachers who had never seen a stock certificate,
swarmed into the big and little stock markets all over
the country. Banks, corporation treasuries, foreign fiscal
agents emptied their cash balances into these blazing
infernos of speculation on margin loans, thus pumping
more oil on the flames. The most explosive element in
this situation was the blow delivered our banking system through the use of the newly popular bank affiliate,
by which a bank could create a kind of satellite corporation through which it could engage in all those dangerous and dizzy adventures forbidden by law to the
bank directly.

Thus our economic system was plunging forward
on a raging sea of debt resting on a thin foundation of
cash and a towering structure of credit, stocks floating
around the exchanges in a hurricane of paper, while
turbulent streams of income poured through all the
shops on Main Street.

A new school of economists told us that the bleak
old world had at last floated out upon a warm and

happy sea called the New Era. Then, on October 29, 1929, the stock market crashed in Wall Street and the Great Depression was on. I can speak with some frankness about it because I attempted at the time, against the advice of unwilling editors, to call attention to this dizzy boom and its inevitable end.

I do not minimize the severity of the depression which followed. Essentially it was an ordinary recession blown into disastrous dimensions by the immensity of the indefensible boom which preceded it. It must be said, in all honesty, that this depression would have run its course perhaps in a year or two were it not for some unfortunate contributing factors. One was the economic crack-up of Europe which preceded our own. The other was the weakness of so many banks because of their bad banking practices. Still another was the magnificent opportunity it gave the Democratic politicians who had been roaming the wilderness since 1920. They went to work with the zeal of crusaders to heap coals upon the depression fires by keeping the alarm bells sounding and whistles blowing over the rising crisis. One dark aspect was that Franklin D. Roosevelt, in 1933 as he took over from Mr. Hoover, had no plans whatever for dealing with the crisis. He appeared as a Saint George in shining armor with his sword uplifted to slay the Dragon Depression—a subject about which he was totally ignorant.

The psychological effect of this depression cannot be overstated. It had something of the appearance of that long-predicted capitalist catastrophe dear to the socialist creed. The frustration of business was almost complete. And into Washington poured evangelists of every known revolutionary philosophy, including some new ones.

It is not necessary to review here Mr. Roosevelt's first term. It was certainly not animated by any coherent economic philosophy. Socialists, communists, fascists and just plain crackpots poured into Washington in 1933, and each got a little something. Mr. Roosevelt himself staked his hopes on two plans. One was spending money. The other was the NRA—the National Recovery Administration—which was in no sense socialistic. It was almost pure fascism. It organized industry under federal auspices—in total defiance of the Constitution—into great guilds or syndicates, in which employers and employees joined in legislating for each organized industry. Uninformed critics called it socialism. It was a crude form of syndicalism. But in the end it blew up in a disorderly explosion of futility without any help from anybody. The Supreme Court unanimously declared it unconstitutional, to the relief of Roosevelt and his advisers and almost everyone else.

The other plan of the first New Deal was to spend money—both tax money and borrowed money. The federal government spent in Roosevelt's first term 25 billion dollars compared with Hoover's expenditures of 14 billions which Roosevelt had denounced. Roosevelt collected only half of his spendings in taxes.

It would not be true to credit the communists or the orthodox socialists with any important part in the confused circus known as the first New Deal. But as the President's first term moved to an end, various radical groups began to get their bearings. The collapse of the NRA—which they heartily despised, correctly branding it as fascistic—played into their hands. It left Roosevelt in a vacuum without any clear policy.

However, there was present in Washington the pink penumbra of the socialist philosophy—politically angry and frustrated reformers, displaced and poorly paid teachers from schools and universities who were disposed to question the eternal fitness of private enterprise, most of them because they resented the low salary scales on which they existed. And there was that swarm of professional and journalistic critics of capitalism of the smart-alec variety who embraced no other philosophy but poured out their scorn on the "bloated bondholder," the "trust magnate," the Wall Street speculator and the crooked politician—all of whom were dramatized, with some justice, in the press as the villains of the depression.

On the outer rim of the aroused proletarians and their bourgeois apostles there was a whole menagerie of new and fantastic preachers of strange cults of every sort. These were neither socialists nor communists. There was Dr. Townsend and his $200 a month for all over 60, Upton Sinclair and his EPIC plan, Sheridan Downey with his Ham and Eggs Every Thursday—who got elected to the Senate in California—Huey Long with his "Every Man a King," Howard Scott and his cult of Technocracy, and many others. All these apostles of change were doing the work of the real socialist revolutionaries, who realized that these wacky groups were promoting a definitive renunciation of capitalism and hastening the arrival of the capitalist catastrophe, which was a necessary prelude to the coming socialist revolution.

Chapter VI

A NEW
NAME
FOR
SOCIALISM

By 1936 Mr. Roosevelt's New Deal had completely collapsed. All his fantastic plans had made no serious impression on unemployment. There were practically as many unemployed in 1936 as in 1933 and far more on relief. The President complained bitterly and justly to his cabinet that "everybody tells me what is the matter, but no one tells me what to do." The politicians were in a state of frustration and ceased to exercise any important influence on events. These events, however, would soon be shaped by a wholly different set of men who were not politicians, but resolute social revolutionaries.

These revolutionaries were not all in agreement. There were radical communists, moderate socialists, half-way socialist reformers and a whole confused army of angry and discontented critics of American business who were not too clear as to the remedy. But this much was clear. The term "communism" was odious to most people and the term "socialism" was only a little less odious. The practical disappearance of the Socialist Party in the 1936 elections made it clear that the label of socialism, as well as communism, no longer had any value in selling their philosophy. The socialist revolutionary took the advice of Edmund Wilson who urged years before "to take communism away from the communist." Indeed, they proceeded to go further and take socialism away from the socialists. They did this by giving it a new brand label, far more enticing to the pragmatic American. They called it The Planned Economy or Social Planning. So far as I know, the launching of this idea in any effective way came in 1932 with two books. One was called *A Planned Society* by George Soule[12] of the *New Republic*. The other was *A New Deal* by Stuart Chase.[13] By 1936, just as Roosevelt's first New Deal was in a state of confusion and frustration, these two books attracted the attention of the Leftists and, with the collapse of the Socialist Party, this new flag—a new and more alluring socialist flag—was hoisted.

It was at this point the really formidable drive to make America into a socialist society began. It is important, therefore, that we follow with the closest attention the launching of the plan. I repeat that the term "socialism" or "communism" or "collectivism" was aban-

[12] New York, Macmillan, 1932.
[13] New York, Macmillan, 1932.

doned. George Soule began his book with the assumption that capitalism had definitely failed. He knew no method of rebuilding it. Instead, the government should take over the task of planning the economic system. He proposed an Economic Planning Board. Stuart Chase in his book called it a Peace Planning Board. Charles Beard suggested a National Economic Council, with industrial syndicates under the parent body to direct our industrial and agricultural activities. Soule approved of this plan. He did not think capitalism would be got rid of suddenly. He thought we should seek to direct the rise of The Planned Society out of the ashes of the capitalist system. The next step—after taking over the great industries—would be to organize society as a whole. The State must control society as a great economic unit—a vast economic apparatus operated under the direction of the federal government.

The Economic Planners pointed to Russia as a model, though of course there were some who gagged at Russia's rugged methods. Assuming the failure of the old system, they turned to create a Planned Society. But they urged we did not have to wait for the total overturn of capitalism. Our government could begin by taking mills, mines, land and electric power. But "every step must be a step away from capitalism." Managers would be paid as such and profits would go into the national treasury, to be reinvested according to plan. Soule described his Planned Economy as creeping briskly over our society under the leadership of the Planners. And he was sure this could all be brought about without violence. The capitalists themselves, one group at a time, would be taxed out of the picture. The rulers would cease to have faith in their own principles. *"The citadel crumbles from within; it is not merely stormed from without."* [14] (Italics added.)

Stuart Chase's book, published at the same time, promoted the same set of ideas and hopes. He called it the New Deal, but he advocated, like Soule, the Planned Society—"The drive of collectivism leads to control from the top." He conceded it may entail a temporary dictatorship. He was not sure we could make communists or fascists out of the present crop of American engineers, bookkeepers and electricians. He was for what he called a "third road" which "moves slowly, cautiously and away from accustomed habit patterns." But he expected it would emerge gradually. Here is how it would function:

> "At the control switches of the nation stand perhaps one hundred thousand technicians . . . responsible in the last analysis for the food and the very lives of 120 million people. *If they should all desert the controls for as much as a few hours we should be done for.* These men have an altogether realistic perception of cause and effect . . . Increasingly they are becoming aware of their importance in the scheme of things." [15]

Chase adds that the scientific attitude "tends to color the minds of industrial managers (not owners), professional men and women, skilled workers, particularly machinists and electricians, teachers, particularly in universities." They have three grievances against our system: It impoverishes them. They have no economic

[14] *A Planned Society,* p. 281.
[15] *A New Deal,* p. 177.

security. "They are not satisfied with the capitalist way of life, frustrating as it does their integrity and canons of workmanship." Chase did not think labor would revolt. The torch must be carried by another class, one hitherto unknown to history. Who? Who but "the men and women who have grasped the hand of science." [16]

How will this begin? Chase thinks we should begin by taking over the railroads, coal, steel, power, oil and other resources. That, indeed, is quite a chunk to start with. And what will this celestial abode resemble? Chase's answer, written in lyrical phrases in 1932, sounds strangely hollow in 1955: "Here, O boys and girls who come to me and ask what you may do to serve the commonwealth is opportunity as great, as thrilling, as any generation, save"—save what? Chase concludes: "As any generation save, perhaps, in Russia has ever known." [17]

And what is the promise? "Thousands of exciting careers . . . not only in the central planning and regional planning agencies—the Staff—but also in the administrative boards—the Line. Back of you will stand the intelligent minority, perhaps organized into a new political party, converted and pledged to the Third Road." [18] Here is the plan for the gaudiest, dizziest bureaucracy ever dreamed of outside Russia.

The great importance of these two theses of Chase and Soule lay in the fact that they got rid of the ugly label of socialism and much of its repelling gibberish. The Planned Economy! Here was a brand label which had in it a powerful pull on the imagination of the

[16] *Ibid.*, p. 179.
[17] *Ibid.*, p. 219.
[18] *Ibid.*

pragmatic American. Before them lay the broken pieces of the capitalist system, now in grave disrepair after four years of Mr. Roosevelt's New Deal. What could be more plausible than the proposal that an unplanned economic society had run off the track in a shocking way? What more seemingly logical than to turn now to orderly, intelligent planning of our society to enable it to work at full speed and without pauses? The appeal of this new label for socialism was almost miraculous. Now it was possible for even conservatives to be social-ists under a new name. The stigma of Marx and Lenin and of socialism and communism was taken off the package.

Chapter VII

REVOLUTION

AND

THE

INTELLECTUALS

This idea has an immense and explosive appeal to a certain type of intellectual. I do not, of course, imply that all persons of large intellectual calibre are seduced by this fuzzy philosophy. I do say that it is an occupational disease of intellectualism. Silicosis is an occupational disease of coal miners, but only a fraction of them succumb. It is probable that the vast majority of so-called intellectuals are well-balanced, sober-minded people who do their work with interest and satisfaction without any disturbance in their mental balance. One frustrating condition, of course, is the comparatively small financial return to workers in the field of the mind—teachers especially, as well as journalists and a large number of writers and run-of-the-mill scientists. There are among these persons a number who resent the disparity in the salary of the professor of philosophy or history compared with the unlearned member of the board of trustees or the school board who earns as much as half a dozen teachers put together. There is something wrong, they feel, in a society which pays $50,000 to a bank president and only six or seven thousand dollars to a professor of economics or English poetry.

There is another mental disturbance involved in this problem. It is sometimes the case that a gentleman who knows how to split an atom or even compose a majestic symphony or write a book of poems of passion, may suppose that he also knows how to construct a model society on some new and gentler plan—and rule it as well. One does not run into many authentic poets who assume that their peculiar power enables them to split the atom or even understand what it is. But as every man in a free society is a citizen, he is at liberty to suppose that the role of citizenship itself qualifies him to rule or, even more, to divert himself in the intoxicating pastime of social architecture.

There is nothing new in this. The dynamic appeal in this idea cannot be understood unless we realize that it is not new and that it antedates Marx by many centuries. The building and direction of the State throughout the ages has been considered a department of philosophy by the philosophers. It is a fact that all during human history, society has consisted of the herd and the shepherd—the masses, and the monarch and lords and warriors who understood the methods of acquiring power. The intellectual, if he was present, served the warrior. There were in most early civilized societies intellectuals who gagged at this rule of the knight and the soldier. Hence they dreamed of the perfect commonwealth where they would rule the herd. The herd would be better off, not because it acquired the right to rule itself, but because of the benevolent mastership of the philosophers.

The earliest evangelist of this school was Plato. He sketched in his *Republic* the outlines of the perfect planned society. There would be no private wealth. All would be rich since all would have an equal "allotment" of leisure, merry-making, visiting, drinking and begetting children. There would be the Workers who would produce, the Warriors who would defend the city and the Philosophers—the Guardians—who would "bear rule." No inhabitant would take part in government until he was 35 or 40; and after 50 the more intelligent would be chosen as guardians and would occupy their time in philosophical studies. They would form a monastic order, live in seclusion and never touch silver or gold. The artisans would have no share in government because they could not become philosophers. Here, therefore, in the early years of the ancient world, was the dream of the Dictatorship of the Philosophers.

Perhaps the most famous of these mythical heavens was Sir Thomas More's *Utopia*. More was a philosopher and a dreamer who went to the block because he refused to yield to the policies of Henry VIII after the monarch's break with Rome. In his treatise, More introduced us to a mythical navigator, Raphael Hythloday, who discovered a fabled communist island society called Utopia. The people divided their time between agriculture and industry, the whole product going into warehouses, whence each family could withdraw its share of goods. There would be no hoarding, no covetousness, no gold or silver. All ate ample meals in a common hall to which the diners were summoned by the trumpet. Children were cared for in nurseries. Every 30 families chose a magistrate and each ten magistrates chose an Over-magistrate who served for life and who chose a philosopher-prince who also ruled for life.

Not long after More, Sir Francis Bacon created another earthly paradise ruled by a "philosopher king." Bacon, described as "the wisest and meanest of mankind" came up with a solution closely akin to that of More, who could be justly described as among the wisest and kindest of mankind. Bacon, in retirement because of his conviction of bribery, conjured out of the mystic seas his own island—New Atlantis. The center of this paradise was Salomon's House, a laboratory where chosen students pursued the search for truth and constituted the *ruling aristocracy of the island.*

About the same time other Utopias sprouted—one in Italy and one in Germany. Thomas Campanella, an Italian monk, brought up from the deep a fabled island discovered by a fabled mariner—the perfect society known as the City of the Sun. Here the people were poor, because they possessed nothing, but rich because they wanted for nothing. The State was supreme and its powers were deposited with an *aristocracy of learning.* Here there was progressive education, to be discovered later by John Dewey. The City had seven walls on which were presented pictorially the seven regions of knowledge, so that the little children would inhale their education painlessly without going to school as they strolled the streets. Johann Valentin Andreae came up with a German version of a communist heaven known as Christianopolis. The Rulers of the City—the Commissars—would determine the needs of all for a given period whereupon the mechanics and farmers would produce them under the direction of the Commissars—representatives of religion, justice and learning—the Commissariat of the Philosophers.

The last quarter of the 18th century and the first quarter of the 19th produced the most extraordinary eruption in history of what have come to be known as Eggheads. The Egghead has been defined by Louis Bromfield as a character who pretends to the title of philosopher—a sort of professional intellectual—dedicated to the theory that the Eggheads are the appointees of destiny who will bring something known in the intellectual trade as "security" to a creature known as the "common man," in return for which he will deliver himself to the management of a society managed by the Eggheads. The society of the Eggheads today embraces communists, socialists, rudimentary fascists, along with their wives and certain rich men's sons and daughters, and even some corporate vice-presidents.

Near the end of the 17th century, the Age of Reason was dawning and presently the Age of the Machine would appear. The shape of the Western world would change and a newer and somewhat more rational breed of social architects would also enter the arena of ideas. But the communist philosopher with his enclosed commune would persist for a long time. What is more, the philosophers would in some instances desert the realm of fiction and begin to set up their enclosed heavens peopled by actual human beings, while others would toy with the idea of transforming great commonwealths into communist gardens of abundance and peace. Rousseau was telling France that private property was plunder and that all must return to the golden age of nature. Babeuf was teaching pure communism applied to a whole existing society, where production would be carried on by government agencies whose officers would determine what each family would have. All would dress alike and children would be taken from their parents at an early age to be instructed in the principles of the communist State.

There still were, however, dreamy philosophers making blueprints for small communities like Utopia. Étienne Cabet was a lawyer who entered the French Chamber of Deputies. He invented a mathematically precise heaven called Icaria, a commonwealth divided into 100 small provinces, each province into 10 communes. The capital of Icaria would be in the exact mathematical center. Each block would have 15 houses. The streets would be straight, the sidewalks covered with roofs of glass. The State would own all agricultural and industrial units and manage all. All would dress alike, including the women. Education would begin at five and end at 18 for boys and 17 for girls and all would work until they reached 65. Literature would be rigidly censored. Of course the inhabitants would choose their governors from among the technicians. These would constitute a Dictatorship of the Technicians. Cabet felt his plan would require 50 years to complete in France. Blocked in that highly policed country, but impatient to begin, he decided, in 1848, to launch his experiment in—of all places—Texas. He actually gathered 1,500 pilgrims for his paradise. The Icarians, however, turned out to be human beings and began to behave as such. The first victim was harmony and Icaria dissolved.

It taxes belief to witness these masterpieces of credulity launched by men of great intelligence, but all convinced that the erection and direction of society is the peculiar mission of the philosopher, with a growing admission to the ranks of power of persons vaguely defined as technicians. What could be more bizarre than the career of Count Henri de Saint Simon, who was born in 1760? He insisted he was descended from Charlemagne. He inherited a large fortune which he lost. But he nursed his dream of glory. His valet was instructed to wake him each morning with the admonition: "Arise, Monsieur le Comte. You have grand deeds to perform." He fought in the American Revolution and later, during the Commune in Paris, was thrown into jail as an aristocrat. In his cell his ancestor Charlemagne, he informs us, appeared to him with an interesting challenge. The august shade called his attention to the fact that in all history no family had produced both a great hero and a great philosopher. Charlemagne reminded St. Simon that he, the dead emperor, had given the family its great hero. Now St. Simon must become its heroic philosopher.

Thus urged, St. Simon plunged into speculation and made a fortune. He then studied philosophy and, to enrich his knowledge of man, he lived successively as a profligate, a pauper, and a gentleman of fashion. After this he settled down to remake the world. He wrote three volumes, the *Industrial System,* the *Catechism of Industry* and the *New Christianity.* There must be a new order that would guarantee *jobs for all under the men of science.* The striking fact about this scheme was that it attracted at once a whole rabble of professors, writers, poets, journalists, philosophers and some engineers and politicians. The president of the Constituent Assembly of France became a member, as did De Lesseps, the builder of the Suez Canal. The École Polytechnique became its stronghold.

In time St. Simon drifted out of the leadership, which passed into the hands of Enfantin, an erratic exhibitionist, who abolished the institution of marriage in favor of free love, which ended the movement. The end, however, is sufficiently grotesque to be mentioned. Enfantin and twoscore leaders, some of them men of distinction, retired from the world to live an aesthetic life as a sort of monastic order, studying astrology and geology. But after a brief go at this, the order dissolved and Enfantin returned to everyday life and amassed a fortune.

These men were not fools. Many were men of great intelligence and some were driven by generous dreams of a better world. But there is a little screw somewhere near the center of the intellect which holds all its functions together in harmony so that a man may dream, yet dream within reason. When that little screw gets loose, the imagination, the reason, the senses of order, balance and proportion, seemingly begin revolving in contrary and eccentric orbits with amazing results. Shakespeare described it in Ophelia as "sweet bells, jangled out of tune." These curious philosophic warriors might be described as "good brains, jangled out of tune." It would be easy to name a dozen, even a full score, of eminent men—some of them in business—in the affairs of America these last dozen years who would most certainly have been members of St.

Simon's entourage and might have persisted even when Enfantin took over.

This was not an 18th-century disease. There are many among us today deeply infected with it. Take the case of Henry Wallace, a perfect example of a devotee of the cult of "intellectualism." He has toyed in his time with almost every religion, having, in his search for peace, probed Buddhism, Confucianism and other cults. He told the Federal Council of Churches that perhaps we should be moving toward something like the theocracies of old. He finally got tangled with a curious old wandering mystic named Roerich, who concocted a hash of yogiism and various other Oriental cults. A whole collection of well-to-do American mystics gathered around Roerich, who was addressed as the Guru. One of the disciples, a Wall Street broker, built a temple for him—a $1,100,000 apartment house in which the first four or five floors were dedicated to the ministrations of the Guru. Roerich decided to go to Asia to establish a new state in Siberia. And to make the journey financially possible, at the expense of the American taxpayer, Wallace, as Secretary of Agriculture, commissioned this grotesque old faker to go to China to collect wild grass seed. But some difficulties intervened and while Roerich was in Asia, Wallace backslid and fired him. This curious adventure, which has the flavor and odor of the enterprises of St. Simon and Enfantin, took place here in our own time and country in a group led by a man who was Vice-President of the United States, and missed becoming President by only a few votes.

Associated with St. Simon was a far greater intellect—that strange recluse, Auguste Comte. He had served for a while as secretary to St. Simon, but in later life denounced him as a quack. Comte is known chiefly as the founder of the philosophic system called Positivism—the central idea being that philosophy must concern itself with knowledge based exclusively on experience. Comte had an intellect of the first order, but he was subject to periods of dark melancholy in one of which, at the age of 30, he threw himself into the Seine from which he was rescued—to resume his philosophical studies. But Comte, the recluse, felt called on to venture upon the reconstruction of the work-a-day world of which he knew little and which, indeed, he despised, and from which he gradually withdrew. Almost all the data on which this work-a-day world is based lies outside the mind of the recluse and embraces a formidable array of forces including economics, law, the table of weights and measures, the laws of gravity, the science of management and, above all, a knowledge of mankind. Comte had a system of investigation which he called *Hygiene Cerebral*. His method was to retire into complete seclusion, avoid people, newspapers, scientific and economic reports and devote himself to reading religious and political tracts. For setting about the reconstruction of society this was hardly a method to be recommended. Yet, little informed of the play of human, economic and political forces, he withdrew into complete seclusion to prepare a blueprint for the reconstruction of society.

Rejecting religion, he felt he had to find a substitute for it. He created a spiritual image called Humanity to replace God as the center of adoration. He sought to duplicate the images, sacrifices, rituals and external forms, including prayers, in his new church. One of his critics described his new religion as the Catholic

Church minus Christianity. There would be a hierarchy, an officialdom, a priesthood, an elaborate series of feast days to excite the devotion of the faithful. But running through his whole system was the central idea that the *rule of the people belonged to the philosophers* who would be the clergy, as well as rulers, in this new order.

It is a fact the significance and influence of which cannot be ignored, that at the base of all these schemes of social reconstruction—from Plato to Marx—ran this idea of the *Soviet of the Intellectuals.* The attraction of this idea is nowhere more sharply illustrated than in the impression made by Comte's philosophy on John Stuart Mill. But in the end the pragmatic Mill had to repudiate Comte, and his comment on this morose philosopher is most revealing. Mill said frankly that he "agreed with him [Comte] that the moral and intellectual ascendancy, once exercised by priests, must in time pass into the hands of philosophers, and will naturally do so when they become sufficiently unanimous and in other respects worthy to possess it." But, added Mill, "when he exaggerated this line of thought into a practical system, in which philosophers were to be organized into a kind of corporate hierarchy" [19] invested with that kind of spiritual ascendancy possessed by a religious hierarchy, he could follow him no longer. He saw in it *a scheme which would invest the State with a despotism which would extend to every part of society.*

This pinpoints sharply the curious evil in this strange theory. First, it contemplates a society fully planned in its operations by an organized body of philosophers and administered by them. Of course this

[19] John Stuart Mill, *Autobiography,* Harvard Classics, Vol. 25, p. 133.

proposal ignores the solid fact that such a society or any other, when set up, will be administered not by philosophers but by politicians who possess the special talent for getting and holding power. The philosophers who created this formidable engine of power will probably all be in flight from the country or in jail.

The most illuminating episode in this weird history is to be found in our own country in that curious madness called Fourierism. Charles Fourier (1772–1837) was a traveling salesman in France. He discovered that the earth was passing out of its infancy and he contrived a plan to usher in 70,000 glorious years for mankind, when lions would be used as draft animals and whales would draw vessels through the seas. He proposed to reorganize society into groups called Phalanxes—small communities of from 400 to 2,000 inhabitants each. A central building—the phalanstery—would be surrounded by a purely agricultural community. Workers would dine in a central hall on meals prepared in a community kitchen. Each inhabitant would produce enough from his 18th to his 28th birthday to support him in comfort the rest of his life. This society would be headed by a Unarch and all the Phalanxes would be united under an Omniarch residing in Constantinople. The millennium, however, would not appear for ten years.

The most amazing aspect of this movement was not its weird simplicity, but that it crossed the ocean to America and commanded the support of many of the foremost writers and artists in this country. Its most noted convert was Horace Greeley, founder of the New York *Tribune*, who ran for the presidency against Grant and polled 2,834,000 votes to Grant's 3,597,000. Greeley was recruited into the Fourierist movement by Albert Brisbane, a journalist who was engaged by Greeley to write for the *Tribune* about this new fenced-in heaven. Another convert was Parke Godwin, later a famous associate editor of the New York *Evening Post*. Charles A. Dana, editor of the *Sun*, and George Ripley, literary editor of the *Tribune*, also enlisted for this new paradise. Societies were formed to promote the new great dream and held a national convention in 1840 in which Greeley, Dana, Ripley and others took a leading part. The intellectual center of this movement was the Transcendental Club in Boston, the most exclusive rendezvous of America's intellectual world. There Nathaniel Hawthorne, the novelist, William Ellery Channing, the great Unitarian divine, George Ripley, literary critic and encyclopedist, John S. Dwight, poet and music lover, Ralph Waldo Emerson and, among the women, Elizabeth Peabody and the famous and beautiful Margaret Fuller, breathed into the movement the inspiration of their flaming souls and their wide intellectual influence.

However, this enterprise required more than a soul. Hence George Ripley bought a 200-acre tract not far from Boston, and on it the first Phalanx was formed, known as the Brook Farm Institute of Agriculture and Education. Here its happy denizens would get employment according to taste, free education, medical care, baths, dancing and music, lectures and discussions and —of course—very short working hours. And hovering over its destinies were the master spirits Greeley, Godwin, Dana, Emerson, Thoreau, Hawthorne, Ripley,

Lowell, Whittier and others. Hawthorne has idealized this adventure in his novel *The Blithedale Romance*. In addition to the Brook Farm Phalanx others were started at Red Bank, N.J., and one or two other spots. The phalanstery at Brook Farm was nearing completion when it was destroyed by fire. Thus the great adventure vanished—ended by one fire.

It is an interesting fact that this curious blueprint of an earthly heaven fired the imaginations of what might be called the intellectual élite of America. Ralph Waldo Emerson wrote to Carlyle in England: "We are a little wild here with numberless projects of social reform—*not a reading man but has a draft of a new community in his waistcoat pocket.*" It was the same in England. Social conditions cried aloud for reform and many serious and practical men were busy at that. But there was the same gaudy, giddy experimentation in transcendental economics, played up in song and poetry. Wordsworth wrote:

> "Bliss was it in that fair dawn to be alive,
> But to be young was very Heaven! . . .
> To meditate with ardor on the rule
> And management of nations, what it is
> And ought to be; and strove to learn how far
> Their power or weakness, wealth or poverty,
> Their happiness or misery, depends
> Upon the laws and fashions of the State."

And Shelley mourned:

> "The seed ye sow, another reaps;
> The wealth ye find, another keeps;
> The robes ye weave, another wears;
> The arms ye forge, another bears."

The problem, in which there was at least a grain of truth, having been stated, the next step is a leap "into the wild blue yonder." The root idea at the bottom of this long history of reckless blueprinting from Plato to Karl Marx, Aneurin Bevan, Henry Wallace, and their disciples such as Dr. James Conant, Dr. Robert Oppenheimer and the essayists of the floundering *Nation*, the *New Republic* and the *Daily Worker* is that social planning is the peculiar mission of the poet, the playwright and the novelist, the scientist and the teacher generally. Obviously I do not imply that this disease afflicts all writers, teachers and intellectuals. I merely suggest that the members of these crafts, some of them dissatisfied with their share of the social dividend, are apt to offer a peculiarly sensitive incubation to these giddy ideas. In the last 20 years in America this disease has run like a scourge through our colleges and journals of opinion. The bursting egotism of the intellectual collegian, sensitive to this subject and supposing that his diploma confers on him authority to seize the world by the scruff of the neck and shake it into good behavior, may be seen in the following chant by one of our most intrepid New Deal intellectuals as he left the campus at Columbia and charged into the battle with his war song on his lips:

"I am strong.
I am big and well made.
I am sick of a nation's stenches.
I am sick of propertied czars.
I have dreamed my great dream of their passing.
I have gathered my tools and my charts.
My plans are finished and practical.
I shall roll up my sleeves—and make America over."

The singer of this song was young Mr. Rexford Tugwell, who inevitably found himself, with his charts and his tools, as Under Secretary of Agriculture under Mr. Henry Wallace, who himself was equipped with no end of fantastic charts and tools. But this brash and exultant proclamation of authority and capacity to blueprint and operate the economic life of a vast nation is not confined to the young collegian. Recently Dr. Vannevar Bush, president of the Carnegie Institution, informed us that what this country needs is a "natural aristocracy"—a minority of eminent intellectuals who will plan our political and economic lives. This curious cult of the "Soviet of the Intellectuals" has persisted through the centuries—this fatuous notion that because a man knows how to split an atom, hunt down viruses, write an ode or compose a symphony he is best qualified to undertake the rule of nations. There can be no doubt that the intellectual descendants of that curious company of brilliant quacks who presided over the rise and fall of the great phalanstery at Brook Farm can still be found in quantity in the groves of Harvard today.

Chapter VIII

THE

GOSPEL

ACCORDING

TO

MARX

The Fourierist adventure was the last of those gaudy Utopian dreams to flourish in America. While the philosophers, professors, poets and other literati dallied with this nonsense, a much more formidable philosophy was being kindled in Europe. The machine age created a new landscape which was enticing hordes of peasants into the cities and their slums. Long hours, grimy mills, the hazards of cumbersome machinery and the intervals of depressions and booms all created a variety of human problems for a new school of social reformers. There was no place in this new machine age for these enclosed Utopian heavens. Socialism, which had been a dreamy cult, began to have a sharper relevance to the new age.

No one with a grain of the humanitarian spirit could support the thesis that all was well in Western Europe and, for that matter, in the new mill cities of America. The new socialist reformers began to talk about revolution, which would bring the workers into the streets of European cities in a bid for political and economic power. This new demand was for a transfer of the instruments of production and distribution—the economic apparatus of society—to the hands of the State.

Karl Marx became the great apostle of this faith. He said crisply his task was not the setting up of Utopias. And, in time, with his friend Engels, he produced what would become the gospel of socialism—the *Communist Manifesto*. This famous document contained a number of mere humanitarian and other reforms, such as bringing wasteland into production, improving the soil, free education, an end of child labor. But the heart of the *Manifesto* was not in these reforms but in its revolutionary demands. These called for (1) abolition of private property; (2) abolition of inheritance; (3) confiscation of the property of immigrants and rebels; (4) state ownership and operation of transportation and communications; (5) a heavy graduated income tax; (6) a gradual extension of the transfer of the instruments of production to the hands of the State.

This was the first concrete platform of the modern socialist revolution. Harold Laski has said correctly that Marx created the first positive philosophy of socialism, which had hitherto been a mere vague and angry protest against social abuses. Here was a doctrine, simple and appealing at once to the intellectual dreamers and the dispossessed poor. The doctrine had a powerful humanitarian appeal to minds disturbed by poverty, injustices and grave social inequalities. The older customers for Utopian heavens were quickly fascinated by the new dream. Horace Greeley, who had helped finance Brook Farm and had hired Brisbane to write about Fourierism, now engaged Marx to explain the new socialism to his readers. Later, of course, the *Tribune* would fall into very different hands and become the organ of reactionary Republicanism and the champion of big business. But, in recent years, it would seem that the disturbed ghosts of Karl Marx and Horace Greeley, revisiting the glimpses of the moon, rise to hover like troubled shadows over the sanctum of that obfuscated journal.

Marx had summoned the workers to unite—"You have nothing to lose but your chains." He was talking about violent revolution. But just before this, another and more rational evangelist had launched his crusade for suffrage reform. John Stuart Mill, who had flirted with the socialist movement, declared the ballot had opened the way to rational reform. And many years later Engels, before he died, conceded that great revolutions could be effected more quickly by the ballot than by violence. Marx himself is said to have come to the same conclusion before his death. Socialism became a reform movement, its purpose being to kill capitalism one limb at a time. Even Karl Kautsky observed that capitalism can grow into socialism, which became the root idea of the gradualists, as they were known on the Continent, and of the British Fabian movement. Here it is labeled properly "creeping socialism"—that is, the piece-by-piece liquidation of the system of private enterprise, replaced by socialist enterprises until the private enterprise sector of the society crashes under the weight of its socialist partner.

It is a fact, of course, that socialism made little headway in the United States. From 1912 on, Socialist Party candidates polled several hundred thousand votes for the presidency, but never enough to constitute a real threat. Eugene V. Debs polled nearly a million (919,-799) votes in 1920, and Norman Thomas polled 728,-800 in 1932, the year of the depression crisis. After that, the Great Depression, instead of advancing the fortunes of the socialists, practically reduced their party to utter futility. The Party polled only 187,000 votes for President in 1936, and 20,189 in 1952. One might assume that the Depression actually marked the Socialist Party as one of its greatest victims. But we must never ignore the tremendous importance of the fact that while the depression wrecked the Socialist Party, it breathed new life into socialism. Strange as it may seem, the socialist movement got under way in America on an amazing scale as the Socialist Party faded out of effective life.

It is not possible to overestimate the significance of this curious twist of fate—the death of the Socialist Party and the rise of socialism as a movement in America. With the practical demise of the Socialist Party, the socialist philosophy has come to dominate the political and economic development of the United States on a scale so broad and at a gait so rapid as to give to it the dimensions and pace of an authentic revolution. The explanation is obvious. The word "socialism" conjured up before the mind of the American the total load of the socialist revolution. The socialist leaders were honest in the frank exposition of their whole purpose which

was to enthrone the central State as the political ruler
and economic employer of everyone. The American
people, despite their loyalties to one party or another,
had no illusions about the politicians who ran them—
corrupt, selfish, wasteful, crude, incompetent. The
havoc they had wrought upon city and state governments was a favorite theme with journalists of every
school. The idea of installing them not only in our political activities but in all our vast economic agencies ap-
palled the average informed American disgusted with
the incompetence and rascality of the politicians. They
had no taste for handing over to them all the great instruments of production and distribution of wealth.

A people who were deeply moved by the slogan
"Throw the rascals out" in our city and state and federal
governments, exhibited no hospitality for the suggestion
that the rascals be invited into all the industrial and
economic installations of the nation. Yet, today in America, with the demise of the Socialist Party, the socialist
philosophy has come to dominate the society and government of the United States on a scale so broad as to
become the foremost challenge to our whole philosophy
of organized life and our liberties as well. Of course the
professional politicians remain in power, corruptly
armed as never before. The Socialist Party has practically disappeared, but the professional politician, interested in power, has become suddenly enthralled with
the weapons put into his hands—the vast flood of government taxes and borrowed funds to be spent on jobs
for the faithful. Thus this old-fashioned politician, with
these socialist weapons in his artillery, is enabled to
purchase the support of businessmen as well as workers,
the growing legions of revolutionary teachers, writers

and publishers and, of course, the numerous minority groups dedicated to the interests of various pet nations and the several types of one-worldism. And so while the old-fashioned socialist disappears, this new brand of socialism, under the false label of Social Planning, is taken over by the professional politicians of both parties.

In what has gone before, I have sought to clarify a group of factors and principles which are essential to a clear understanding of our present difficulties. I have set it down as a fact that the American Republic, after nearly a century and a half of its history, has been subjected to a profound and revolutionary change.

In expounding this thesis, I have attempted to make a clear picture of that thing we call the State—which is the corporate soul of the population in an actual political structure. The State uses a thing called government as the instrument of order and control. Government is an apparatus of power—power to make the rules and to enforce them. Government itself, therefore, throughout history has been a problem of the first order, for it is the institution which possesses the corporate authority to rule its citizens wisely and justly and freely or to exploit and oppress them. This danger arises from a thing called the Administration—the organized collection of human beings who at any given time has in its power the apparatus of government. The great problem of civilized man has been to erect a *government over a society, in the hands of an Administration he can control—a government which will have the power to protect the citizens but without the power to exploit or oppress them.*

The solution of this problem, we have seen, was attempted throughout history with varying forms of

government, but never with any real or lasting success.
The problem was settled in a very real sense only in
America. And this was done, as we know, by breaking
up the apparatus of government into a number of separate machines or instruments of power. To describe it as
it was up to 1932, there were 48 separate state governments—48 small republics—absolutely independent and
getting their sovereign power from a charter prepared
by themselves. They were supreme in their own domin-
ions. There was an overall republic, with highly limited
power—the federal republic—which could do nothing
save what the states specifically authorized in the Constitution. The vast power of sovereign authority over the
lives of men was deposited in no one central government. No one group of administrators had in its hand
anything more than a fraction of the sovereign authority of the republic. The purpose of this, as I have stated
several times here, was to give the people all the government a free society required, but so disposed that no
one powerful central administration could gather all
powers into its hands and use them to oppress the people.

What is more, the greatest care was taken that no
alteration in this great institution could be made, no
powers taken from or given to either the states or the
central government without a formal change in the
great charter itself—the Constitution. And this continued to be the form of the American government until
the year 1937, when Mr. Roosevelt began his second
term. In the years since that time, this republic has been
dismantled from top to bottom and a wholly new kind
of government—a government of usurped powers—has
been set over us. Finally, it was humanly impossible

for any administration to set up a socialist government in the United States because of the Constitution. A socialist government could be established only by formally amending the Constitution and conferring vast powers upon a central government which it did not possess under the Constitution, and by liquidating those sovereign powers of the states.

Chapter IX

SOCIALISM
AND
THE
CONSTITUTION

This brings us to the central point of this study. It must be obvious to any honest mind that a socialist society cannot be organized and conducted by the federal government under our Constitution. The powers of the central government are all derived from the Constitution and these are set out with the greatest particularity. The extent and meaning of these several powers had been defined over and over by the Supreme Court. There is no one sentence in the Constitution that would authorize the federal government to socialize our medical facilities, to regulate or finance our schools, to engage in industrial and mercantile enterprises, or to carry on any of that multitude of activities which have, as a matter of record, brought the federal government into almost every kind of business in one degree or another. There is no way in which this can be done save by a bold political iconoclast who despises law, constitutions, restraints of every sort—the only limitation being such as might arise from an angry population. This did not appear, of course, first because the whole structure of our government was hidden behind the masquerade of war and the orgy of spending fantastic billions borrowed to fight wars to save "democracy" in Europe and Asia, while it was trampled on here in America.

I have said that the great limitations on the federal government were specifically set down in the Constitution. The Constitution gave it no broad grant of powers. Its functions were set out specifically in Article I, Section 8. There is a general grant to lay and collect taxes, duties and excises. Then there is a careful enumeration of the purposes for which taxes and duties may be levied. These are to:

Borrow money on federal credit.

Regulate commerce with foreign nations and between the several states and the Indian tribes.

Establish uniform rules for naturalization and bankruptcies.

Coin money, regulate its value and the value of foreign coins, and fix the standards of weights and measures.

Punish counterfeiters of coin and the securities of the United States.

Establish post offices and post roads.

Establish a system of copyrights and patents.

Provide for courts inferior to the Supreme Court.

Define and punish piracies and felonies on the high seas and make rules governing captures on land and sea.

Raise and support armies, but appropriations for such purposes can last for but two years.

Maintain a navy.

Make rules governing land and naval forces.

Provide for calling the militia to execute the laws of the Union, suppress insurrection or repel invasion.

Exercise exclusive jurisdiction over the Nation's capital and places purchased in states for federal purposes.

Make all laws necessary and proper for carrying into effect the foregoing powers, and all other powers vested by the Constitution in the government of the United States or any department or officer thereof.

There is nothing in the Constitution which authorizes the Congress to engage in anything save those functions which are enumerated in the Constitution. The whole purpose of the framers of the Constitution, as well as of the men who ruled our government for nearly a century and a half was to bring into existence a government that possessed all the powers necessary to defend the nation from foreign enemies and to guarantee to all the citizens certain great fundamental rights of freemen, and to leave to the states—the several small republics—the powers essential to the government of a free people.

in history

Thus, for the first time the great powers of government were no longer committed to the same set of hands or to the management of a single administration. All the powers needed to govern a free people were present, but so arranged that these powers could not be used on any broad scale to oppress them. Here was government—not one huge and formidable government machine in the hands of a single administration, but a great central authority which would protect the people against external enemies and regulate a few and highly limited number of social arrangements on a national scale, while far the greater powers of government were left with the states—13 smaller separate republics. Here was the perfection of government for free men. And it remained on this model for 144 years—the admiration of the world and a beacon light to men everywhere who yearned for freedom.

It will not do to say that times have changed, that the social and economic life of the people in a machine age calls for a government equipped with more formidable powers than those enumerated in the Constitution. If this be so, then the means of increasing the powers of the federal government are specifically stated in the Constitution. This can be done only by constitutional amendment—by going back to the states with a plea for more power. This was done on several occasions. On one such occasion an almost fatal blunder was made when the Constitution was amended to permit the imposition by Congress of a federal income tax, without limit. The federal government never had the power to raise excessive taxes under the Constitution as

it stood for 123 years. Indeed, it was severely handi-
capped. To correct this situation the Income Tax
Amendment was adopted. The great blunder in this in-
cident was the failure to put a drastic limitation on the
amount of the tax permitted. Some argument could be
made for a severely limited income tax, but none whatever for such a tax without limit. However, many men at
the time felt that there was already a sharp limitation in
the Constitution that would automatically limit the tax
—that is, the very limited number of subjects over which
the federal government had authority. But the granting
of unlimited taxing power was a crime against our system of government of tragic dimensions, as we shall see.

The second crime which completed the war on our
Republic was to come much later—and we shall consider it shortly—through the infamy of a collection of
judges packed onto the Supreme Court for the specific
purpose of performing an operation on the Constitution
by judicial decree. Unable, as they knew, to change the
Constitution by lawful amendment, the radical elements then in possession of the mind of President Roosevelt hit upon a plan to pack the Supreme Court with a
group of radical judges who could be depended on to
perform the necessary surgery on the Constitution—
which they did and continued to do with shameless
abandon.

The socialist society which these elements envis-
aged required a powerful central government that
could assert its authority over every sector—indeed
every county or neighborhood—in the land, with total
power over the economic life of the people. It could
own the railroads, all electric power, all the great instruments of communication. It would assert ownership

over all the great natural resources of the nation—coal, iron, copper, oil. It would own banks, all the agencies of saving and insurance. It would own or regulate all our farms and mines, operating what it believed suited its purposes and subjecting the others to its regulations. It would assert the right to tax and tax, demanding the bulk of the profits from our industries and a heavy cut on whatever income a private citizen might have. It would be a government endowed with such vast and compulsive powers that once any political or economic group got possession of its dread machinery, no man would dare lift his hand—save the darling of some opposition party pledged to operate the socialist monstrosity better.

To bring on the socialist society in the United States the first blow was struck—43 years ago—by a nation that had no suspicion of the gravity of the breach it had made in our Constitution by the Income Tax Amendment. It would be years later that the second great assault would be made. It must be clear to the reader who has followed these pages that the federal government under our Constitution did not possess any powers required to organize a socialist society. This had never been questioned in 145 years. And the socialists of the United States up to 1937 realized this fact. No one has defined our system more clearly, as we have seen, than one of the darling philosophers of our modern socialist revolutionaries, the late Charles Beard.[20]

Beard clearly recognized the all-important fact— and he did so with approval—that "no faction or political party could get control of the whole government."

[20] See quotation from Beard at pp. 37-38.

Yet a very small group—which would become danger-ously powerful—insisted that it could get into its hands at one time not only all the instruments and weapons of government but all the vast installations of the eco-nomic system, thus creating on these shores a monster of political and economic power. Once this monster came into the hands of any ruling group the last feeble spark of freedom would be extinguished.

It was the considered judgment of our people and their leaders that government itself—however essential to orderly and free life—could be, if not curbed and con-trolled, the instrument of tyranny. Now a new school had arisen which proposed not merely to dismantle the Constitution and bring at last all the powers of govern-ment to the center, but to add to their political power the control of all the engines of economic life.

An honest man, bent on making this into a socialist society, might well offer an amendment to the Constitu-tion running about as follows:

> The authority of the federal government shall extend to every form of economic action in the nation, including the right to acquire by purchase or condemnation any or all types of industrial or agricultural or mercantile enterprises, including all forms of transportation, electric-power generating and distributing systems and any other type of economic enterprise; provided the government compensate the owners justly; and that all such forms of economic enterprise not so conscripted by the federal government may be operated by private persons but under such plans and methods as may be determined and promulgated by the Congress.

Preposterous as this proposal may seem, this is precisely what the Planned Society—the Collectivist State —or the Socialist State, if you please, calls for.

Chapter X

THE

DARK

ALLIANCE

Despite all the endless care exercised by the framers of the Constitution, and the judgments of the Courts for over 148 years, these revolutionary elements in the United States found a way in which to complete their perversion and subversion of the Constitution without submitting these radical changes to the states —the only authority empowered to make changes in the Constitution.

The stock market crash came in 1929. Thus was ushered in what came to be known as the Great Depression, the causes of which we have already examined. The crash was followed in the next four years by a widespread flight from investment, a growing army of unemployed, the gradual undermining of our banking system, a rising tide of radical opinion in our labor unions, academic circles and certain political spheres. President Hoover struggled painfully against this current of angry agitation, but as his term neared its end, his power to do anything passed from his hands. His defeat in 1932 was clearly foreshadowed and, with the election and inauguration of President Roosevelt, the whole banking and economic system was swept into collapse.

This was in 1933 and it was as of this date and amid these scenes that President Roosevelt inaugurated an incredible series of adventures that defied almost every sentence in the Constitution. In general, the President brought into existence a collection of commissions and bureaus empowered to take over the direction, supervision and in some cases the management of vast areas of American industry and finance, utterly outside the limits of his constitutional powers. The central organism in this fantastic circus was the National Recovery Act (NRA) and the Agricultural Adjustment Act (AAA). Every department of American business was compelled to organize under the stewardship of the federal government into what were called "authorities" which were empowered to make laws governing every phase of industry. A more shocking defiance of the Constitution could not possibly be imagined. It literally liquidated vast areas of state power and set up a wholly new system of legislative bodies in the "authorities" which all employers and labor bodies were compelled to join, each in his own field of trade. These "authorities" were empowered to make the most extensive regulations respecting hours of work, prices, profits, relationships with labor and suppliers, etc. It was, although few Americans realized it, modeled on Mussolini's corporative State. It was not socialism or communism. It was pure fascism on the Italian model.

A similar operation was organized for the farms in the AAA, directed by Henry Wallace, under whose guidance food and crops were destroyed to create scarcities and thus raise prices. The "slaughter of the little pigs" became the classic example of this insane scheme. The AAA was empowered to make the rules for farming, farm labor, crop controls, prices—all supervised by a vast bureaucracy which was authorized to compel compliance by rugged powers buttressed by the ability to reward complying farmers with generous government checks. The farm and the farmers became wards of the federal government on a scale which even the socialist agricultural arrangements later instituted in Britain never attempted.

There were other agencies and laws reaching almost every department of American industry and commerce which, when they began to function, literally tied the American economy in a fantastic strait jacket. The Administration acted as if the Constitution had ceased to exist.

Then in May, 1935, the Supreme Court declared the NRA unconstitutional in a unanimous decision, even the "liberal" Justices Brandeis, Cardozo and Holmes joining in the decision. After this, in a succession of decisions, the Court invalidated the Agricultural Adjustment Act, the Guffey Coal Act, and various similar adventures of socialist and fascist tinge. And this episode set off a violent debate about the Constitution and the Supreme Court, whose judges were scornfully dubbed the "Nine Old Men."

In the midst of these controversies over the Constitution, President Roosevelt was reelected by an enormous majority, carrying every state save Maine and Vermont. Despite this, he entered upon his second term with grave misgivings. The whole program of the first term was in ruins, not only because it was declared unconstitutional but because it didn't work. It was reprobated by the conservatives. What was more serious for the President, it had found little favor with the leftists —not because it was unconstitutional (which it was) but because it was fascist or syndicalist in essence. And finally there stared him in the face those vast legions of the unemployed. There were still, at the beginning of his second term, ten million working people unemployed. There were families comprising 15 million persons on relief, which would swell to over 20 million in another year. The only thing which sustained the President was the enormous sums of money appropriated, out of heavy government loans, to spend on relief activities of all sorts. But there was no recovery.

There was no recovery because no effort was made to produce recovery. There was no intelligent examination of the defects in the system of free enterprise. Instead there was a succession of proposals for socialistic or collectivist schemes and endless interference in the machinery of the private enterprise system which created in the minds of investors and managers a deadening feeling of frustration and fear. There were, of course, many evils in private business. But the end that should have been held constantly in view was the correction of these evils and the revival of industry. Instead business, the businessman and the investor were set upon by the government, not to reform abuses, not to make private agencies of production and distribution work more effectively, but to punish them and discredit them and, in some cases, to milk them or destroy them.

This situation produced the golden moment for the socialist revolutionaries. What had gone before was a confused hodgepodge of measures—some socialist, some fascist, most of them mere devices for keeping people on the dole. The student of this epoch must never lose sight of this fact—that the so-called first New Deal was not in any sense a communist or socialist operation. It had actually found little favor with the communists or socialists, in spite of the fact that large numbers of them managed to insert themselves into the numerous collectivist agencies set up in 1933.

The crackpot schemes had failed; most were liquidated. And recovery remained aloof. The socialist cabal, now well schooled in the stratagems of a socialist Europe—in Germany, France, Italy and England—saw its opportunity here. They now appeared in Washington to confront a triumphant but frustrated and planless President with a workable plan.

This was the hour of fate for America. We can see now and understand clearly the overall program of the socialist revolutionaries to make a socialist America—without making any *lawful* change in our great charter of freedom, the Constitution of the United States.

It is essential once more to remind the reader that the socialist revolution no longer appears before us under the name of socialism. The cause of socialism is no longer promoted in the United States by a Socialist Party which, as we have seen, once upon a time polled almost a million votes but in 1952 could muster only 20,000. But today the socialist revolution is more vigorous than ever and has actually succeeded in inserting immense sections of its program into the structure of the American government. This was possible, to repeat, because the promoters of that philosophy operate on a wholly different level and have discarded the jargon of socialism and the unpopular socialist label.

To understand this we must recognize that there are in America a variety of groups which pursue various parts of the socialist objective; that they are interested for personal reasons in this or that socialist scheme. The promoters of socialism have different names for the several sectors of the socialist program. They are united in one objective—that the federal government have unlimited authority to do whatever the politicians think is good for the country. One group favors some moderate scheme to promote something called the "good life"—sometimes called "security." Another thinks a large part of all the vast machinery of education should be subject in one degree or another to federal control and support. Others think the federal government should take over the immense field of electric-power production and distribution, first through TVAs and then all other types. Then there are advocates of government ownership of railroads, airlines and steamships, or of state or local ownership of subways and buses. New York City already owns and operates its subway, of course at a staggering loss. Others think the federal government should take over such basic industries as coal, iron, copper, aluminum, oil, etc., or should make the rules under which they are operated.

One or more of these measures is advocated by different groups, while they disclaim any affection for socialism—not realizing that when one group succeeds, the path is open for another. Politicians interested not in socialism but in votes cultivate the support of these various minorities. There are certain powerful business groups which support other schemes, such as the government's staggering and fatal foreign aid programs and its incredible military adventures, because they make the weapons and depend for their dividends on these gaudy international adventures. This is just one example of a powerful minority in business interested in profits and blinded by that to the gravity of their course. They seem to be unaware of the fact that the business they enjoy piles up the taxes and deficits of the federal government and that this gradually moves the government and the society to economic disaster in which these business groups will be engulfed. For a temporary gain they weaken the system at one spot and thus promote the socialist strategy of breaking down one piece at a time the economic apparatus of free enterprise and the political apparatus of republican government. The revolutionaries believe that this will go on until what is left of our historic system will crumble in ruin.

Thus the stage is set for the socialist revolution. The staggering majority received by President Roosevelt in 1936 installed him with immense power. But he was without a program. That was the moment for which the collectivists had been waiting.

We have seen how George Soule and Stuart Chase, in two sly volumes, had revealed the strategy for selling socialism under a new and attractive brand label— *The Planned Economy.* Shortly after Roosevelt's second inauguration, a new group appeared. There was a sense of apprehension in Washington at the time at the immense sums that were being spent by the government, much of it borrowed money. At this critical moment a new batch of philosophers turned up with an answer to these misgivings—at the very instant when President Roosevelt was complaining that "no one tells me what to do." This happy and welcome idea came, like the Chase and Soule proposals, in a book called *An Economic Program for American Democracy* by seven young Harvard and Tufts scholars.[21] It was, of course, not a program for American democracy. It was a program for American socialism. Its central theme was that a government, unlike an individual, can borrow and spend indefinitely without fear of bankruptcy. When Roosevelt was elected in 1932 the federal debt, after 143 years, was $19,487,000,000. After denouncing Hoover as a spendthrift, Roosevelt had borrowed almost as much money in four years as the total national debt after 143 years. Both Roosevelt and his Congress were gravely troubled about this. But this little volume pointed out that *a government, unlike an individual, can borrow and spend indefinitely without fear of bankruptcy*. A government debt, it said, was not like a private debt. A government borrows from its citizens. The debt is in fact owed by the citizens. And as the citizens own the government, the debt is really due to the citizens. A government debt, these gentlemen argued, is therefore due by the people to themselves. No matter how big the debt grows, they assured us, the actual impact on the citizens and government is negligible—unlike a private debt.

The apostle of this sly philosophy was Dr. Alvin H. Hansen of Harvard. When this small book, written

[21] Vanguard Press, 1938.

by Dr. Hansen's disciples, appeared, the doctor was promptly brought to Washington and installed in the Federal Reserve Board as the economic philosopher of this new dispensation. And most of the book's seven authors turned up in posts in various New Deal bureaus. Now Roosevelt had a luminous guide through chaos: (1) The American economic system planned and directed from Washington, and (2) an endless flow of funds to spend, supplied by endless borrowing.

Chapter XI

THE

ASSAULT

ON

THE

CONSTITUTION

But, as we have seen, *one barrier stood in the way of these socialist adventures—the Constitution of the United States.* The federal government—a government of severely limited powers—had no authority to operate a socialist State. A socialist society requires a powerful central State, equipped with immense powers to own and operate or plan the activities of the whole industrial and commercial system. This is impossible under the American Constitution. To carry out this program would require the most fundamental alteration in the Constitution. It would call for a powerful central government on an almost unlimited scale and the liquidation on the same scale of the sovereignty of the states.

Article V of the Constitution provides how it may be amended. There are two methods: (1) The Congress, by a vote of two-thirds of both houses, may submit amendments of the Constitution to the sovereign states. (2) The states, through action of their own legislatures, can call a convention to submit amendments, but this must be done by two-thirds of the states, and amendments may be submitted at such a convention. But in either case the amendments must be ratified by three-fourths of the states through the action of either the legislatures or conventions called for the purpose. Nothing could be clearer than this. But our collectivist revolutionaries, realizing they could never succeed by lawful and constitutional measures, hit upon another plan. And Roosevelt happened to be precisely the man to do the job for them. As his second term began, he was in a boiling rage against the Supreme Court of the United States for wrecking his unconstitutional first New Deal.

The Supreme Court is empowered, under the Constitution, to "interpret" the meaning of the Constitution where questions of judicial differences appear. It had, according to its time-honored practice, interpreted the Constitution to mean what its framers wanted it to mean, and declared Roosevelt's first-term acts unconstitutional—in the most important case by unanimous decision. There was, therefore, but one course open to the revolutionary cabal in Washington. It was a plan to change the Constitution, literally to wreck the whole fundamental structure of the American government, not by orderly process as laid down in the Constitution, *but by judicial interpretation.* The plan for accomplishing this lawless aim was welcomed by Roosevelt almost as soon as it was presented to him. This was the infamous scheme "to pack the Supreme Court."

Roosevelt sent the plan to Congress in early February, 1937. The Supreme Court had for many years been made up of nine justices. Roosevelt's plan provided that the President would be empowered to appoint an additional justice for every sitting judge over the age of 70, provided the total number of justices would not exceed 15. The target aimed at, of course, was to name one New Deal judge whose vote would nullify the decision of one member 70 or over. There were six judges 70 or over—Hughes, Van Devanter, McReynolds, Brandeis, Sutherland and Butler. There were three others between 60 and 70. Had this bill passed, immediately six judges would have been appointed to nullify the votes of any six justices over 70 then sitting. And there was the further proposal, which the Congress accepted, to permit justices to retire at 70 on full pay, the purpose of which was to expedite the disappearance from the Court of those judges objectionable to Roosevelt.

The purpose of the whole scheme, of course, was to get a bench that would uphold as valid Roosevelt's fantastically unconstitutional measures. Congress refused to adopt this assault on the Court, it being defeated by an outraged coalition of Democrats and Republicans. But in the end, Roosevelt's objective was achieved. Assured of retirement on full pay, and weary of the venomous attacks that had been made on them, the older justices began to resign. The following bowed out—Justice Van Devanter in 1937, Sutherland in 1938, Butler (died) and Brandeis in 1939, Hughes in 1941. With the appointments of Hugo Black, Stanley Reed, Felix Frankfurter, William O. Douglas and Frank Murphy, Roosevelt had a majority of the justices and a Court the radicals could count on to perform whatever surgery was needed on the Constitution to open the way for the collectivist State.

Once a Supreme Court subservient to the President and the new collectivist revolution was installed, the job was easy. It was simply necessary for the Supreme Court to give new and utterly different meanings to *four words* in the Constitution—meanings those words had never had in the preceding 148 years. The four words are comprised in the terms "general welfare" and "interstate commerce."

The term "general welfare" was clearly understood for a century and a half. I have listed the specific powers conferred upon Congress. Congress was empowered to collect taxes, etc., "to provide for the common defense and *general welfare of the United States.*" That did not mean that Congress could tax for any project which might seem good to Congress to "promote the general welfare." It did not refer to general welfare in the sense the word "welfare" is now used—as a system of handouts to the indigent, etc.

The Constitution declared that "to provide for the common defense and general welfare" of the United States, Congress can do certain things. It then proceeds to enumerate these powers. It could borrow money, regulate foreign and domestic commerce, punish counterfeiters, establish post roads and post offices, provide for copyrights and patents, establish courts, make laws affecting the high seas, declare war, raise armies, provide a navy and for calling out the militia. These are the powers specifically delegated to Congress to "provide for the common defense and general welfare."

The Constitution did not leave to any vague doubts what the Congress could do for the general welfare. The section provides, in the same way in the same sentence that Congress could "provide for the common defense." To implement this, it included in the enumeration of powers that Congress could raise armies, organize a navy and make rules for governing the land and naval forces and could call out the militia. And in the same way it could provide for the general welfare by doing the other things enumerated—borrow money, regulate foreign and domestic commerce, punish counterfeiters, etc. In short, Congress could provide for the common defense and the general welfare, and the Constitution stated specifically what it could do for these purposes. And Congress' powers are restricted to these grants. The Constitution did not by any stretch of language mean by general welfare that system of handouts which have been in vogue during these last 20 years. It did not and does not mean that for the "general welfare" the federal government can support state schools or build roads in the states or carry on any other activity not specifically granted in the Constitution itself.

Alexander Hamilton himself, arch protagonist of powerful government, recognized sorrowfully the extent to which he had failed to win for the federal government the powers he sought. To those who complained the Constitution granted too much power, he replied:

"The power of Congress . . . shall extend to certain enumerated cases. This specification of particulars evidently excluded all pretension to a general legislative authority, because an affirmative grant of special powers would be absurd, as well as useless, if a general authority was intended." [22]

Actually, the question arose in the very first Congress. A bill was introduced to pay a bounty to Cape Cod fishermen and a subsidy to farmers—two perfect New Deal projects. James Madison, one of the framers of the Constitution and a member of the Congress, spoke at length in the debate on the bill. He said:

"If Congress can employ money indefinitely to the general welfare, and are the sole judges of the general welfare, they may take the care of religion into their own hands; they may appoint teachers in every State, county and parish and pay them out of their public treasury; they may take into their own hands the education of children, establishing in like manner schools throughout the Union; they may assume the provision of the poor . . . Were the power of Congress to be established in the latitude contended for, it would subvert the very foundations, and transmute the very nature of the limited government established by the people of America."

Thomas Jefferson, who has been kidnapped as the patron saint of the radicals of today, wrote in 1817 that the grant of power to promote the general welfare did not give Congress any additional or unlimited power to legislate for the general welfare. On the contrary, he said, "it was restrained to those powers specifically enumerated."

These views were adopted by Congress, which re-

[22] Federalist No. 83.

jected the proposed Cape Cod fishery bill, after which Jefferson commented:

> "[This] *will settle forever the meaning of this phrase, which by a mere grammatical quibble, has countenanced the general government in a claim of universal power.*" (Italics added.)[23]

This interpretation of the general welfare clause continued to be accepted by the Congress and the Courts alike for all the years of the Republic up to 1937. On January 6, 1936, Justice Owen J. Roberts, who had crept a long way with some of the so-called liberal justices, wrote what would seem to be a definitive statement of the historic meaning attached to the general welfare clause in the Constitution. The AAA sought to establish the federal government as the overlord and director of American farms. The Court held it unconstitutional. Justice Roberts wrote in his decision:

> "Until recently no suggestion of the existence of any such power in the federal government has been advanced. The expressions of the framers of the Constitution, the decisions of this Court interpreting that instrument, and the writings of great commentators will be searched in vain for any suggestion that there exists in the clause [general welfare] under discussion, or elsewhere in the Constitution, the authority whereby every provision and every fair implication of that instrument may be subverted, the independence of the individual states obliterated, and the United States converted into a central government exercising uncontrolled

[*] Letter to Albert Gallatin, 1817.

political powers in every state of the Union, superseding all local control or regulation of affairs or concerns of states." [24]

The other two words which were conscripted to alter the meaning of the Constitution were "interstate commerce." The Constitution gives Congress the clear right to "regulate commerce with foreign nations and among the several states." The Constitution is based on the theory that each state will regulate commerce and industry within its own borders. But when a citizen of one state engages in commercial transactions with citizens across the border of another state, the framers of the Constitution realized that in such a case, where a question of rights or law or regulation was concerned, that was "interstate commerce" and, as such, ought not be left to either of the states concerned, but was a matter of federal control and interpretation.

The meaning of the word "commerce" was clear. It is not synonymous with the word "business." It does not mean "manufacture." It means "trade"—the "exchange of goods, productions or property of any kind." Thus it is defined in dictionaries of our own day. Congress was not given the power over "commerce." It was limited to regulation of *interstate commerce* only. When a producer manufactures goods or a farmer grows crops these products are not in commerce until the producer offers them for sale or transportation. They are not in interstate commerce until they are contracted for and actually move across state lines.

The Courts never wavered, throughout our history, in their clear understanding of the term "commerce"

[24] U.S. v. Butler, 297 U.S. 1 (1936).

and of "interstate commerce." It meant trade; and it included transportation as an inevitable function of trade. They understood precisely what the Constitution meant and why the terms were used. The states were sovereign republics, united in one great overall republic. The states retained full sovereignty to manage their own internal affairs. But a problem arose out of the process of trade between the citizens of one state and those of another. There had to be an impartial umpire and rule maker when the citizens of one state began to do business with citizens of another and to transport goods across state lines. That field of regulation and that alone was properly committed to the Congress. And that authority the federal government got, not from any inherent sovereignty of its own, but through a direct grant of power in the Constitution from the states. In 1871 an attempt was made to show that commerce included manufacture. Justice Field rejected that theory and held that interstate commerce in a commodity begins *"whenever a commodity has begun to move as an article of trade from one state to another."* [25] (Italics added.)

Of course, the subject became troublesome when large corporations began to spread their activities over many states, and when the growing evil of corporate monopoly began to make itself felt. Communities and smaller interests clamored for action by the federal government against the growing power of the trusts, and for every abuse there was a band of organized reformers calling for action against their own pet abuse. They all overlooked the fact that while there was the problem of curbing predatory or anti-social man on one side, there was also the continuing great adventure, at-

[25] The Daniel Ball, 10 Wallace 557 (1871).

tempted in America, of keeping in leash the abuses of too-powerful anti-social government.

But the Courts always, to their credit, kept foremost in mind the meaning of the Constitution and in decision after decision on questions involving "interstate commerce" kept to the true meaning of the clause. At the same time, it is not true to say that the Courts were insensible to the abuses of the corporation and of corporate monopoly. There were cases in which they tried to reach the abuses of monopoly and yet keep within the terms of the Constitution which the Court was set up to defend.[26]

Also, it is not true that our country was helpless against the so-called "malefactors of great wealth." Federal and state power, between them, were adequate when wisely used. It is a fact almost forgotten that, in the end, the war upon the old Standard Oil Trust was won by a State Attorney General in a suit in a state court in Ohio, which ordered that trust dissolved. But it is important for the student of our Republic to remember that among all the social evils—many committed by unscrupulous businessmen—which aroused the concern of generous-minded people, one of the greatest evils that had plagued the world throughout history was the evil of Big Government. That problem we had solved here, so far as it can be solved.

[26] For cases showing the Court's historic interpretation of the commerce clause, while at the same time attempting to reach the abuses of monopoly, but always within the terms of the Constitution, see particularly Chief Justice Fuller's opinion in the "Sugar Trust" case (U.S. v. E. C. Knight & Co., 156 U.S. 1, 1895), Justice Harlan's opinion in the Northern Securities Co. case (No. Securities Co. v. U.S., 193 U.S. 197, 1904), and Justice Day's opinion in the Child Labor case (Hammer v. Dagenhart, 247 U.S. 251, 1918).

The most persuasive fact on this point is the position of the Democratic Party itself when it nominated Mr. Roosevelt in 1932 in the midst of the depression. Calling attention to the depression then moving swiftly to its crisis, the Democratic Party announced its program. *It called for a drastic reduction of government expenditures by at least 25 per cent; abolishing useless commissions and offices; a budget annually balanced; a sound currency to be preserved at all hazards; a competitive tariff; federal loans to states to aid in reemployment; expansion of the federal construction program on legitimate federal works to create work; unemployment and old-age insurance; financing of farm mortgages and development of the farm cooperative movement and enactment of every possible lawful measure to aid the farmer—but always being careful to keep within the Constitution; an impartial enforcement of the anti-trust laws; regulation of holding companies which sell securities in interstate commerce; various other reforms—but always stressing the limitation that their efforts would be applied to malefactors and abuses that appeared in interstate commerce; and of course repeal of the Prohibition Amendment.* They also urged the states to adopt measures within their authority to deal with the liquor traffic. There were other planks, but always the greatest care was taken to recognize the limits of federal power and the importance of acting within the framework of the Constitution.

From all this, we can draw the rational conclusion that as of 1932, when Mr. Roosevelt was elected President, there was absolutely no serious break by either party with the great fundamental basis of our Republic as we have described it in these pages. There were differences between Republicans and Democrats on matters of policy within the framework of the Constitution. There were certain marginal areas of constitutional law in which various agitators for sundry reforms and interests sought to commit the government on questionable adventures. There were, indeed, certain differences between various groups of politicians on the true interpretation of some constitutional texts and principles. But there was no conscious repudiation anywhere, until after 1933, of the most clearly understood fundamental principles of our Constitution and the Republic it was framed to guide. And the platform on which Mr. Roosevelt was elected in 1932 is the most convincing proof of this fact.

Chapter XII

FOUR

MAGIC

WORDS

With the advent of the new justices appointed by the President to the Supreme Court from 1937 onward, those four words in the Constitution we have been considering—"general welfare" and "interstate commerce"—took on wholly new meanings. And it was thus that the collectivist revolutionaries tortured and twisted the Constitution—without any change by means of its lawful process for change—to legalize all the unconstitutional projects of the collectivist New Deal.

Among the powers delegated to the federal government was the authority "to regulate commerce with foreign nations and among the several states and with the Indian tribes." As we have seen, a long line of decisions had determined clearly that the word "commerce" referred to trade—the sale, transportation and delivery of goods. We have seen that the authority of the federal government over commerce did not begin until goods moved across state lines.

To illustrate how far afield this new Court went, it must be clear that a small clothing manufacturer making clothes within a state and neither shipping nor selling them outside the state, is in commerce, but by no stretch of words is he in "interstate commerce." In the case of Friedman-Harry Marks Clothing Company, in 1937, the Court held that the business of making clothes must be considered as a whole—it must be looked on not as an activity by one small manufacturer, but as an industry in which thousands of big and little producers are engaged in a number of states. Oddly, this had never occurred to any Supreme Court justice in 148 years. Therefore, said the Court, even a small intra-state manufacturer, operating wholly within a state, must be considered in interstate commerce because there are countless others in the same business in a number of other states. The industry must be considered as a unit. If this is true, there is no commerce which is not interstate commerce. Justice McReynolds, in a dissenting opinion, said: "A more remote or indirect interference with interstate commerce or a more definite invasion of the powers reserved to the states is difficult, if not impossible, to imagine." [27] In the previous year, in a decision affecting the coal industry, instead of a clothing company, Justice Hughes had concurred in an opinion invalidating the Guffey Coal Act and laying down precisely the same principles as Justice McReynolds. Yet,

[27] NLRB v. Friedman-Harry Marks Clothing Co., 301 U.S. 58 (1937).

after this, he concurred in the opinion in the case of the Marks Clothing Company.

Then in 1942 the Supreme Court literally wiped out state boundaries as a limitation on federal power. What could be more essentially an internal operation within a state than a loft building in a New Jersey city? In such a building one of the tenants was engaged in the manufacture of clothing and a large part of its product was sold outside the state. This one firm was clearly in interstate commerce. But in this case, Justice Frankfurter, for the Court, held that not only was the clothing firm in interstate commerce, but the building in which it was just one tenant was also in interstate commerce and thus subject to federal legislation. And because the building was in interstate commerce, the man who ran the elevator was also in interstate commerce as well as the women who washed the windows. Fantastic as was this finding, Frankfurter declared it did not exhaust the extent of federal "interstate power." [28]

If this government is a government of "limited and delegated powers" as has been held time and again throughout our history, from what source did the Congress suddenly derive this power? It gets its powers only from the Constitution. No such power in 150 years was ever delegated by the Constitution or claimed by Congress. Now, suddenly, Justice Frankfurter and his recently appointed New Deal justices, usurped the most fundamental powers of the nation and proceeded to confer powers on the Congress that no Congress or Court had ever claimed. In a later decision this Court held that this same authority applies to porters, elevator

[28] A. B. Kirschbaum v. Walling, 316 U.S. 517 (1942).

operators and watchmen in another office building.[29] If there is anything in this world that is utterly local and out of even the "stream of interstate commerce" it is an elevator operator in a local office building who travels up and down from one floor to another rather than back and forth across state lines.

Whatever power these new judges lacked under the "interstate commerce" clause, they squeezed out of the "general welfare" clause of the Constitution. The grant of power in Article I, Section 8 of the Constitution "to provide for the common defense and the general welfare of the United States," as we have seen, did not mean that Congress could do *anything* which in its opinion would contribute to the general welfare. The Constitution took great care to make this clear and actually to enumerate the things Congress could do to "provide for the general welfare"—borrow money, regulate commerce among the states and foreign nations, coin money, establish post offices, declare war, raise armies and a navy, and several other acts which were not left to guesswork but were specifically enumerated.

There had never been any pretense by Congress that it could do whatever seemed to it good for the general welfare. It could do only those things enumerated in the Constitution. But the new Court proceeded to give legality to clearly unlawful constitutional acts by the Congress by twisting the "general welfare" clause to mean that the federal government could pay subsidies to farmers, give handouts to the indigent, support schools and pay teachers in the states, build hospitals, provide medical care and support all sorts of activities

[29] Borden v. Borella, 325 U.S. 679 (1945).

clearly within the province of the states—all because they were designed, in the opinion of any passing Congress, "for the general welfare" of the people.

Of course, this distortion would not have been possible if years earlier our people had not made the fatal mistake of passing the 16th Amendment to the Constitution permitting Congress to impose income taxes without limit. There had been agitation for some time for a federal income tax, which never got anywhere. But as it became stronger, the 16th Amendment was offered, strangely enough, in what they thought was a completely objectionable form by the enemies of the income tax, and opposed by its friends. Senator Nelson W. Aldrich offered the amendment believing it would be defeated and thus end the agitation. Sereno Payne, who offered the bill in the House, denounced it from the floor, and Cordell Hull, the leading advocate of income taxes, denounced the measure as a fraud. Thereafter, to the amazement of everyone, the amendment was approved by the states with unparalleled speed. It became part of the Constitution just as President Wilson was being inaugurated as President of the United States. Thus the enemies of the law proposed a constitutional amendment in its most objectionable form permitting the federal government to impose income taxes without limit, expecting it would be defeated. They actually offered a plan for *unlimited income taxes* in order to defeat a proposal for a four percent income tax.[30]

[30] The claim is made by the apostles of what is called the "new constitutionalism" that the first step in expanding the power of the federal government was made by the sword in the Civil War. This is, of course, without any base in history. There was not a line in the

After the passage of the 16th Amendment, the federal government had the power to impose an income tax in any amount determined by Congress. But no amendment was passed then or since in any way enlarging or increasing the number of purposes upon which the federal government could spend the money thus collected. The first income tax levied was one percent on incomes of $4,000 and over, with a surtax of from one percent to six percent on incomes starting at $20,000. However, the power to tax without limit was there, although it was used sparingly at first. Today we are confronted with tax rates that start at 20 percent on the lowest incomes and rise to confiscatory proportions —as high as 91 percent on incomes over $300,000. The Income Tax Amendment, of course, would never have had a ghost of a chance for passage if it had been believed that rates even one-fourth as high as these were contemplated. Sixteen years after the passage of the Amendment, the federal government was taking roughly four percent of our national income. Today it takes 25 percent and even this is insufficient to meet its tremendous expenditures. Hence it turns to borrowing billions on a fantastic scale to meet its appalling deficits.

Thus we see that our once severely limited federal government has taken into its hands three weapons which it has used unsparingly to change and distort the American Republic completely: (1) The income tax, (2) the vague, unlimited authority conferred on it by

---

Constitution which authorizes a state to withdraw from the Union. The Constitution itself was a solemn pact between the states to form a central government on certain principles, and nowhere is there any provision in the instrument for the withdrawal of a state from the Union.

wholly new definitions of the "general welfare" and "interstate commerce" clauses of the Constitution, and (3) a theory of endless borrowing and debt as a settled government policy.

The machinery of our government was looked upon for 148 years as an agency of power to protect the people in their rights, but was also recognized as an instrument of power from which the people must be protected. This was done by recognizing the great powers of government residing in the state republics, while in the federal government the greatly limited powers delegated to it were divided among three independent instruments of government—the legislative, the executive and the judicial.

But that Republic has ceased to exist. At a superficial glance, it looks the same. The words in the Constitution, save in one case, are the same. The exception is the Income Tax Amendment giving the government unlimited authority to confiscate every man's income and spend it for him. But by a wholly lawless conspiracy between the President, the Congress and the Court, these words—clearly defined over and over for 148 years—have been endowed with wholly new meanings. The chief purpose of this has been to erect a massive central government possessing the power to plan and build and operate socialism in America. The vast and compulsive apparatus of government had been dismembered by our forefathers and its various parts entrusted to a variety of agencies, no one having in any dangerous degree sufficient power to oppress the citizen. Now that immense collection of machinery has been reassembled at the center, not by an amendment to the Constitution, but by the decisions of a group of judges who were put on the bench in a revolutionary maneuver to give to words in the Constitution wholly new meanings—meanings never dreamed of in the preceding 148 years. The great Republic of our fathers has ceased to exist at least for the time being. The state republics, indeed, remain. But the central government by a series of usurpations has assumed new and vast powers—so vast that the champions of this revolution insist that now the federal government has all the authority needed to organize and operate a socialist society.

Chapter XIII

THE

REPUBLIC

IN

CRISIS

To realize the extent of this assumption of powers by the federal government, we have but to look at a comparison of its expenditures in 1927 and 1953. These comparisons are made wholly between peacetime agencies:

Agricultural Department	1927	$ 155,584,000
	1953	3,217,000,000
Commerce Department	1927	30,383,000
	1953	1,063,000,000
Labor Department	1927	9,800,000
	1953	300,000,000
Health, Education & Wel-fare	1927	19,000,000
	1953	1,920,000,000

One interesting comparison is found in the Office of the President. In 1928, Congress appropriated $585,-000 to cover all the expenses of the President's office. In 1953, Congress appropriated $5,783,000,000—nearly six billion dollars. These sums were appropriated to be spent by the President on whatever purposes appealed to him all over the world.

In the 20 years from 1913 to 1932, including World War I, the total expenditures of our government on everything were $84,000,000,000. In the 20 years from 1933 to 1952, the total expenditures were $700,-000,000,000—nearly seven times as much as during the entire history of the government from 1789 to 1933.

But it is not only in the amounts spent—amounts raised and expended under the theory of continuous heavy government taxes and borrowing—but in the nature of the things on which the money was spent that we see how our Republic has been altered. By 1953, the total federal expenditures in a single year had grown to $74,607,000,000. This, of course, included the costs of the Army, Navy and Air Force, but some $21,000,000,000 of it was consumed in a variety of adventures in manufacturing and various civil and economic activities, in which the federal government has no shadow of right to engage under the Constitution. These included all sorts of manufacturing, construction and other economic activities along with the so-called paternalistic activities of the federal government.

It is impossible, of course, to catalogue in a brief space all the diverse activities in which the federal government has engaged as operator, partner or financial backer. European socialists, who worked to transform their societies into socialist heavens, adopted the strategy of building socialism one step at a time—creeping socialism. They saw the advantage of beginning with electric power, finance, transportation and basic materials. A government which controls our system of transportation, of electric power, our iron and coal mines and our banks has in its hands weapons it can use to bring every business enterprise in America under its control. No business can operate for a week without these basic materials and services.

The most important of these invasions has been the government's intrusion into electric power. It began with the pretense of protecting the Tennessee Valley from floods by building huge dams to dam up the river floods. Of course this does not protect the valley from floods. It has actually submerged under a permanent flood a large part of the valley which suffered from these annual inundations. The impounded water is used to pour over huge installations which are operated to generate electricity. Having begun with the Tennessee River, the government spread out to the Cumberland and built a number of giant hydroelectric plants in Tennessee and Kentucky. These provide insufficient power for the valley, so the government began building steam generating plants—11 of them—in Tennessee, three in Alabama and one in Kentucky.

This is not the whole story. The architects of the enterprise gave it a very significant name. They called it the Tennessee Valley *Authority*. The word "Authority" was chosen to mask their ultimate intentions. They have set down in writing that state lines are illogical— that this valley consists of five states and these must be considered as an economic unit, in which all the basic enterprises must be planned and directed by a central authority representing the federal government.

Of course their plans extend to the entire United States and look to the ultimate extinction of the states. Over 2,821 projects in the field of power have been authorized by the government, of which over 2,000 have been completed. These have cost over 12½ billion dollars and more than 7 billion more of federal funds are to be expended.

Indeed the federal government, once a mere central agency to protect the states and to protect the people from the states, severely limited in its area of power, has now become a vast operating administration consuming many kinds of materials and carrying on many business enterprises. It has become a manufacturer and producer and merchant. The House Committee on Government Operations in a report on this subject has warned that "Federal agencies have entered into so many business type activities that they constitute a real threat to private enterprise, imperil the tax structure and are, in many industries, a step toward socialism." It urges that the federal government "keep out of competitive business enterprises." [31]

The government's ownership of wealth has grown on an enormous scale. The House Committee reports that from 1929 to 1948, while private wealth increased by 78.7 percent, government-owned wealth increased 278.5 percent and that in 1948, wealth—that is, property, industry, funds and other forms of wealth in the nation—owned by the government equaled 27.3 per-

[31] 7th Intermediate Report, House Committee on Government Operations, House Report No. 1197, 1954.

cent or over a quarter of the total. The report says: "It is the largest insurer, the largest lender . . . the largest tenant, the largest holder of grazing land, the largest owner of grain, the largest warehouse operator, the largest shipowner, the largest truck fleet operator." [32]

This report lists a number of industries in which the government carries on extensive manufacture:

Rope manufacture	Metal heat treating
Tug & barge operators	Printing
Alcoholic beverages	Warehousing
Scrap iron and steel operations	Power facilities
Coffee roasting	Tire recapping
Box making	Paint manufacture
Ice cream manufacture	Saw mills

And of course, as in all socialist activities, when the government runs business it runs it in the most expensive and least efficient manner. The Army, for instance, insists it is economical to roast its own coffee— nearly 100 million pounds a year. But the Veterans' Administration, which procures some five million pounds a year, buys on a competitive basis a better blend at a lower price. So serious has this particular situation become that as I write the government is considering which of these activities it can curtail or end.

Under our Constitution the federal government has absolutely no authority to interfere in public education in the states. The creeping socialist groups—the socialists, the communists and their various pink satellite allies—carry on an intensive drive to move the federal government into the field of education. They urge

[32] *Ibid.*, p. 10.

federal grants to public and other schools. Their purpose, of course, is to control curricula, teaching methods and the content of education. To do this they have sought to induce the local educational authorities to appeal to Washington for funds. The plan is preposterous. The federal government can get no funds for education or anything else save from the people in the states, taking money from the states and sending it back to the states as if it were a gift from Uncle Sam. Indeed, it is important that American parents understand that the federal government is really one of the greatest enemies of free education. It drains out of the pockets of the people of the states such vast funds for its political, socialistic, war-making and foreign adventures that it is difficult for the state and local governments to collect adequate taxes for their own needs.

Like all the others, this is a creeping invasion. In 1932, the federal government gave $33,402,000 to the states for teacher education. In 1951 it gave $137,355,-000 for teacher training. It distributed $2,550,000,000 in 1951 for general education. It took huge sums out of the states in taxes—and then handed back a fraction for education. The government has no secret hoard from which to conjure taxes. Taxes can come only from the people in the states. And the federal government always takes from the states, no matter what the purpose, more than it returns. It seeks to bribe teachers and parents with their own money.

The central meaning of all this lies in the fact that the nation is in the midst of a creeping revolutionary movement carried on not by guns but by stealth. It would not, of course, be true to say that all our leaders understand this clearly. They move along with the current in which they are caught because it carries them for the moment in the direction of some personal, business or social objective. It is part drive and part drift toward the collectivist State. And many of the leaders, who are mere politicians rather than statesmen, have little understanding of the direction in which they drift.

The intelligent political leader, as we have seen, understands clearly that there is no such thing as a compact majority. There are only large minorities bent on pressing their own special social or economic or political goals. And each of these minorities, individually, may not think of its goals as socialistic. The farmers, for instance, who have received over 6½ billion dollars in subsidies from the government, do not think of themselves as socialists, nor do certain big business enterprises which enjoy huge war contracts from the government, nor many of the workers in left-wing labor unions who are constantly pressing their demands for government control over industry. But it is the politician's job, if he is to remain in power, to coalesce all these minorities into a majority, and with government funds or government favors to buy the votes of farmers, of workers, of business leaders. It is not because they want socialism that these people acquiesce in such betrayals. They just do not realize that each of these adventures inflicts another wound on the free society. The system of free enterprise cannot sustain these huge tolls. It is impossible to collect enough taxes to pay the bills. Hence the politicians who run the show turn to borrowing money from the citizens, from industry and from the banks. This creates a spurious prosperity which can last only until the taxing power and the debt-paying power of the government is exhausted, when the whole degenerate structure will sink down in disaster.

Here is a revolution taking place under our eyes—one step at a time. Each advance into socialism is made possible by some special benefit in money or legislation which will accrue to some gullible group. And once this drift sets in a most astonishing phenomenon appears. *The nation slides unresisting down the slippery grade into socialism without any Socialist Party being implicated in the adventure.*

Chapter XIV

FROM

DEPRESSION

TO

WAR

BOOM

For all this torturing out of shape of our whole constitutional system, there is supposed to be one all-sufficient excuse—a raging, booming prosperity. It is essential, therefore, that the American citizen understand with clarity that this country *has not enjoyed anything remotely resembling a sober and healthful recovery.*

When the American business world sank down, in 1929, into a depression of unexampled severity, that depression could have been of brief duration and of no great depth. I do not say the depression could have been avoided. I have pointed out that our economic system itself is a human mechanism. It is composed of free men, and free men make mistakes and commit sins which can result in economic depressions. The severity of the depression which started in 1929 was due to the abuses that had grown up in our banking system and in our corporate system. The collapse was inevitable and many men who watched the rising orgy of speculation foresaw it. When it came, it was enormously expanded by the failure of our banking system—the abuses of which, in a measure, were later controlled by the passage of an act sponsored by the late Senator Glass of Virginia—an act which Mr. Roosevelt refused to support.

Mr. Roosevelt was elected as a result of this disaster. It was his duty under our constitutional system to do what was necessary to return the *American* economic system to health. But he did not. What we must understand is that, following the banking crash of 1933, *we have never recovered*. Here are the American Federation of Labor's figures on unemployment for Mr. Roosevelt's first two terms:

January, 1933	13,100,000
1934	13,282,000
1935	12,058,000
1936	12,646,000
1937	10,002,000
1938	10,926,000
1939	11,369,000
1940	10,656,000

The slight decrease in unemployment, such as it was, was due to government spending of borrowed money for various improvised adventures. The relief figures are even more startling. In 1932 there were 4,155,000 households on relief with 16,620,000 people.

In 1940 there were still 4,227,000 households on relief with 16,908,000 people.

Mr. Roosevelt had denounced President Hoover for his extravagance in spending on all the expenses of government 14 billion dollars during his four-year term. But President Roosevelt himself spent 25½ billion dollars during his first term and 33 billion during his second term. He had denounced Hoover for a deficit of 3½ billion dollars. Roosevelt's deficit at the end of his second term was *24 billion dollars*. The government's receipts were only 34 billion of the 58½ billion Roosevelt spent in his first two terms. In other words, over 40 percent of the sums spent by President Roosevelt were borrowed. When he took office in 1933, the national debt, after 144 years of the Republic, was 22½ billion dollars. By 1940 it was nearly 43 billion—almost twice as much as the debt in 1933 after 144 years.

It was not until the war was launched by Hitler and Stalin in Europe in 1939 and we, under Mr. Roosevelt's leadership, became the "arsenal of democracy" that any sort of "recovery" appeared. In short, it must be recognized that Mr. Roosevelt and his successor, Mr. Truman, did nothing to return the American economic system to health. What they did was to maneuver the United States into the European and Asiatic wars. By this means, millions of men were employed in the military and naval forces of the country, far more millions were employed in the munitions plants, and most of the cost of this new and dangerous industry was paid for with borrowed funds—a process which continues to the day I write.

Thus, two very grave changes in the nature of the American Republic have occurred: (1) It has for 14 years lived on an unnatural boom created wholly by war and spending on war. (2) It has in that time been subjected to a revolutionary movement the purpose of which is to transform this great nation (a) into a unitary central system of government and (b) into a socialist economic system.

Each of these objectives is evil in its own way. The socialist society is not possible save in a unitary government—a central government asserting vast powers over every phase of social, political and economic life. To accomplish this, our great federal Republic erected on these shores 166 years ago must be liquidated and transformed into a unitary government possessing powers sufficient to establish and manage a socialist society. In the process of establishing these powers, the Republic—the federal Republic composed of sovereign states—must be dismantled. Socialism cannot be operated in a federal republic such as our Constitution blueprints. The federal Republic and the Constitution which sets out its nature, its powers and the powers of the states and limits the powers of the federal government make this impossible.

In order to create a socialist society, our politicians have been perfectly willing to wreck a republic built to insure freedom. This, as we have seen, has been effected by a Supreme Court composed of lawless judges who were named for the specific purpose of giving new meanings to words in the Constitution—meanings never seen in those words in 148 years of the Court's existence.

The raging prosperity which excuses all that preceded it—the distortion of our Republic and our economic system—is a spurious prosperity built entirely on war and war spending and debt. There is no doubt that the nation has "enjoyed" a wide and, in a sense, a lawless prosperity, though there might be some question as to the intensity of the enjoyment. Some 16 million young Americans were taken from their homes, their schools, their professions and jobs. Some 407,828 died; 670,000 were wounded in World War II, plus 34,000 dead and 103,000 wounded in the Korean War.

While American boys were paying in blood all over Europe and Asia, the people at home were in clover. In 1937 the federal government spent 8 billion dollars. In 1941, as we moved into the war, it spent nearly 13 billion. After that the sky was the limit. Government expenditures rose by leaps and bounds until in 1945 the government spent *100 billion dollars.* After that it spent in the neighborhood of 40 billion a year until 1952, when Mr. Eisenhower took office. Since then expenses have been running between 64 and 75 billion dollars a year, with no war anywhere.

But the government, despite these burdensome taxes, does not collect enough to cover its staggering outlays. Here is the record:

A national debt of 22½ billion dollars when Mr. Roosevelt took office after 144 years of the Republic.

A national debt of 278 billion dollars after Messrs. Roosevelt, Truman and Eisenhower! Under President Eisenhower the debt, in a period of peace, has actually increased by 12 billion dollars.

The essential meaning of all this must be obvious to any rational person. The government keeps a diseased prosperity alive by borrowing and taxing, spending most of the money to supply army units all over the world with weapons and material manufactured in American plants employing millions, paying subsidies to farmers, supporting with federal grants all sorts of business and political activities.

Here, then, is a spurious prosperity built on war scares and wars, vast taxes and fantastic borrowing. In the absence of a fighting war this will inevitably come to an end. But, in the meantime, these sums—so vast as to defy understanding—are spent to buy the votes of various minority groups—territorial groups, economic groups, cultural groups, industries depending on war contracts for the armed services and for our giveaway programs all over the world.

While we waste our substance around the globe and expose ourselves to endless conflict, we are confronted with a crisis in the very fundamentals of our own national life. The gravity of this social disease is hidden for the moment from our eyes by the apparent prosperity—a prosperity in which we are trapped, which is devouring our institutions, our philosophy of the free life, and the basis of our well-being, and which has now brought us to the verge of an economic and social crisis whose dimensions can hardly be measured.

In the meantime we have built up, to almost unbelievable proportions, the one great outside threat to ourselves and the world. When World War II began, Russian communism held dominance over 8½ million square miles of territory and 180 million people. Today it holds dominance over *13 million square miles of territory and 800 million people*—almost all of it won with the help and connivance of the American government. And while we spend our substance and our strength to fight the enemy which we ourselves installed in Europe and the Orient, a strange phenomenon appears amongst us. It is all right—in fact, it is highly commendable—to fight an ideology like communism with guns and tanks and planes and soldiers and dollars in Europe, Asia and Africa. But let a patriotic American who believes in and wishes to protect our American Republic raise his voice against the false prophets of this same ideology *inside the United States and inside our government,* and all the forces of vituperation, slander, smear and calumny come down on his head not only from a large section of the press, but from the government itself.

Chapter XV

THE
WAR
WE DO
NOT
FIGHT

The weird adventures of the American government in its global wars and alliances are important illustrations of the desperate efforts of our shortsighted politicians to fight their way out of a depression with soldiers and munitions of war. They did, indeed, succeed in blowing up a spurious and evil prosperity at a shocking cost in human life, human suffering and material values, including a smashing blow at our political and economic system. But the most dangerous menace to America today is not in Communist Russia or Communist China, abominable as these dictatorships are. Nor is it wholly—or at its roots—in the costly alliances with the so-called Western "democracies." These alliances do, indeed, play a role in disturbing the pattern

133

of a rational foreign policy for the United States. But the truly great war—the most destructive in which we have ever been trapped since 1861—is the war inside the United States waged against us by a dangerous alliance of forces within our own borders. The ultimate aim of this alliance is to wreck the American Republic as blue-printed by our Constitution and to establish here a col-lectivist society on the socialist model. The war we should most fear, but do not fight at all, is the war on our Constitution and the Republic which it defines.

Whether or not we can find some honorable escape from the trap that has been set for us in Europe and Asia remains to be seen. Certainly this is not a problem to be ignored. But I insist it is secondary and that what-ever we do in this field must be subsidiary to what we do against the problem poised for us within our own borders. In general terms this problem comprises the following:

There is this plan to transform our own country into a socialist society.

Before this can be done, however, it is necessary to wreck our economic system of private enterprise by subjecting it to stresses and strains that will enfeeble and ultimately ruin it. This would include the strait-jacket of government regulations, the enfeebling ex-actions of crushing taxation and the poisonous stimulus of endlessly mounting debt.

Essential to all this is the purpose of transforming fundamentally our political system as defined by the Constitution, which is totally unfitted for the organiza-tion and management of a socialist society.

As to the plan to wreck our system of private enter-prise, that project has been advanced on an alarming scale. The system of private enterprise, if it is to function at all, must do so under conditions suited to its nature. There is no need to go into these conditions in detail, but it can be said in general that it can operate at its highest efficiency only in a free society. It is a free system, so that any citizen is at liberty to try his hand at the project of organizing, launching and operating a business of his own or in concert with others. It must operate at a profit. Those enterprisers who have the necessary qualifications will succeed. Those who do not will fail. But in general, and over the long pull, no industry can succeed unless it functions in a political and economic atmosphere suited to the special genius of the system.

Of course there will be some adventurers in enterprise who will not succeed, either because of poor judgment, inadequate capital or unfavorable economic conditions. There is no need to grow sentimental over this. It is not nearly so tragic as to plunge a great nation into a war to escape a depression, or to push it into socialism at the cost of its freedom. Capitalism is a system in which every man who has the requisite qualifications may launch his own enterprise and make it go, whether it be a great oil industry or a small village filling station. But he must have the talent for enterprise. It is the men and women who have this special qualification who make possible all the products and all the services and who create all the jobs and all the money income which all the rest of us use to purchase our necessities and luxuries.

No one can reasonably contend that this system is without its defects, as is anything human. No one has seen at close range this side of enterprise more than I have—its defects and the frailties of some of its promoters and managers. Few writers of my generation used more printer's ink calling attention to its weaknesses before the crash of 1929. Aside from certain inherent defects which will be found in any human organization, there were a number of abuses introduced by those who exploited the system and were responsible for the severity of the crash of 1929—and the later and more shocking crisis of 1933.

The only substitute suggested in exchange for the system of private enterprise is some form of European collectivism—Marxian or Leninist socialism (communism), or some other limited form of collectivism. Obviously our system must be protected from the over-acquisitive man. No one can defend the various schemes and corporate inventions which marked the 25 years of the era preceding the Great Depression. These were managed mainly through the abuses of the corporation system. There was none of these which was not susceptible of correction. When the stock market crashed in 1929 and later when Mr. Roosevelt came to power in 1933, the way was open to a repentent and humbled nation to subject our whole system to a thorough housecleaning. Instead we beheld the most incredible and frantic improvisations not to restore and civilize but to cripple and even paralyze business. I was in Washington a good deal in those days and saw the endless ranks of the crackpots pouring into that frenzied city—some of them youthful instructors fresh out of various colleges, some minor and even hungry scribblers on various left-wing periodicals, others weary old architects of various types of social heavens who had grown wan and discouraged offering them to an inattentive people. All now flocked into Washington where they got a hospitable hearing without delay. A number of them were swiftly installed in an office behind a desk, with a secretary and a grant of money and power from the White House.

It is not necessary to remind the attentive reader that almost all these bizarre schemes collapsed and that in the end Washington turned to the oldest, costliest and most wicked of all boondoggles in history—war— with millions of men drafted into the armies, other millions pouring into the war industries, billions of dollars pouring out of the printing presses in the form of government bonds hastily converted into expendable dollars at the banks. We were at war. The depression was over. The boom—the war boom—was on—the oldest known type of boom in history. That boom continues as I write—now 14 years old—still barging along on the same motor power; the same old engine spouting paper dollars, with only a change of engineers, and two terrifying differences: It continues to operate on the war theme when there is no war; and it is running out of gas.

Chapter XVI

THE

REVOLUTION

OF

OUR

TIME

It remains now to sum up in a few pages the essence of this strange adventure in our history and to describe the elements which now provide the power behind it. First, let us sum up in a few sentences the central facts which explain our present plight since World War II ended in August, 1945. These are the points we must bear in mind:

First, the policy through which, after defeating the German dictator, Hitler, we turned over to the Communist Stalin and his successors almost all the fruits of victory.

Second, the shocking series of distortions to which we subjected our Constitution under which our great Republic was governed, as a result of which we have delivered an almost mortal blow to our own system of political rule.

Third, the conspiracy by which communist and socialist revolutionaries, aided by a packed Supreme Court, have set in motion a fundamental revolution in our economic system.

Fourth, the method by which our federal government has bought off opposition by manufacturing a criminal prosperity built on war, whipped up by fears of war, paid for by confiscatory taxes and equally fantastic federal borrowings exceeding 275 *billion dollars* —to say nothing of those 16 million young Americans taken from their homes and their jobs to fight all over the world and of those 1,077,828 casualties.

Fifth, the policy by which, whether there is a war raging or not, we are kept in a state of war fears—of continuing crisis—by entwining our security with the disordered empires of Europe that are supposed to be our friends, that are described as "our noble allies" and that are sinking gradually behind the red curtain of socialism or communism or some other form of collectivism.

Unless we understand these facts we will fail to make any headway against the strange force which has entrapped us in difficulties all over the world and in a shocking state of disrepair inside our own borders. Is there anything that can be done about this? Can we reconstruct the great, free society we have so gravely injured? Certainly we can do nothing until we understand clearly what has happened to us and the nature of the road along which we continue to descend.

Let me illustrate what I refer to as our confusion. In the political campaign of 1952 the Democratic

Party was denounced as promoting socialist ideas and being soft on communists. It was also denounced as cultivating socialist aims here and leading the nation to bankruptcy by its irresponsible spending orgy. These appeals exerted a powerful influence on the electorate and were the chief motives for turning the Democrats out and putting the Republicans in. But what happened after the election? As I write these sentences, our so-called noble allies are putting endless pressure on our government to soften our policy with reference to Russia and to create an atmosphere in which we and our "allies" can resume trade with Russia, China and the whole communist world. What happened when Mr. Truman left the White House and President Eisenhower took over? In Mr. Truman's last two years his expenditures were as follows:

1951	$44,058,000,000
1952	65,408,000,000

When General Eisenhower came into power, the expenditures in his first two years were:

1953	$74,274,000,000
1954	67,772,000,000

In Mr. Truman's last two years the Korean War was being fought. It ended shortly after General Eisenhower entered the White House. While a part of the expenditures for 1953 were planned under Mr. Truman, the spending continued in the new administration notwithstanding the practical cessation of fighting in Korea. It is a fact that in his first two years President Eisenhower spent *32½ billion dollars more* than Mr.

Truman in his last two. I do not record these facts as a mere criticism of General Eisenhower. I offer them as an evidence of what I have suggested above, namely that there is no difference whatever at present between our two parties. I do not indict the Democratic Party as a conscious vehicle of socialist philosophy. I do say the controlling wing of the Democratic Party has opened its arms so widely and affectionately to such an immense part of the socialist philosophy that in all justice it should now be known as the *Socialist Democratic Party*. This transformation is partly the result of the new socialist strategy and partly the result of the immense political advantage there is in these huge budgets of taxed and borrowed funds with which to buy the support of numerous minorities. In the case of the Republican Party, those who now control it have decided that they can be just as good socialists as the Democrats so long as they reject the label, and partly because in their reach for power they feel it is necessary to compete with the Democrats with gifts and a form of socialism in the market place for votes.

What I have been trying to make clear is that the movement at the bottom of all our ills—including our infatuation with war as a remedy for something or other —is a Dark Alliance, a drive getting its power from a number of minorities. At the control switches (a favorite term with our literary and social engineers) are the communist and socialist revolutionaries. They provide the blueprints, the pamphlets, the poems and songs and the fiery energy of the movement. But they are few in numbers and they derive their political energy from a number of social, political, economic and regional minorities who clamor endlessly for government aid of all kinds—laws, appropriations, handouts, favors for teachers who want federal grants, farmers who want to sell their crops to Uncle Sam, businessmen who see in our fantastic federal spending programs for war and peace the world over an endless stream of government contracts and government payments. It is an alliance—a Dark Alliance—the end of which is to disrupt the American system of private enterprise. But along with this, onto the scrapheap of history will go the American Republic. It must be scrapped as part of this revolutionary plan because no communist, socialist or collectivist society can be built and managed under the American Constitution.

It requires no more than a few words to restate in simple terms the thesis of this argument. First, it is essential to understand that our wars in Europe and Asia are mere by-products of one great central assault on our country. The truly Great War—the one which, as I have said, we do not seem to be aware of and do not fight— is *the war on the American Republic*. Strange as it may seem and difficult as it is to believe, we have been building up the vast Russian Communist tyranny in Europe and Asia and have been tearing down our own great constitutional system in the United States.

Early in the game, the leaders in this movement in America realized that the Great Depression presented them with the opportunity to move the United States off into a shrewd plan to erect a socialist society here. The crash of 1929 was taken to be the definitive evidence of the instability of our American economic system—the system of private enterprise—and its inability to provide abundance for all or to escape recurring crises. Certainly that crash was abundant evidence that the

American system of private enterprise could not flourish continuously under the evil influence of those shameful adventures in banking and corporate finance which disfigured the system and ultimately brought on the depression. What was called for was evident—reform—a whole series of corrections by government and business of the evils that brought on the crash. But the various revolutionary elements saw in it the opportunity to kill public confidence in our own system and our own form of government. And by a twist of fate, the man who came to leadership at that moment, President Roosevelt, urged on by that strange collection of men who surrounded him—Hopkins and Tugwell and Frankfurter and Wallace and a whole regiment of lesser red and pink luminaries—was able to install these revolutionary elements in power. Little was done, therefore, to correct the evils which produced the depression. On the contrary, every effort was directed toward completing the ruin on our economic system which was begun by the depression.

The goal was the creation of an American Socialist Republic. But this could not possibly be done under the American Constitution. That Constitution, as we have seen in detail, was framed to erect here a government designed to create a free society. Human freedom was at its base. No such society existed anywhere in the world. Great Britain at the time enjoyed a system more nearly approaching a free society than any other, but it was very far indeed from that truly free republic which our Revolutionary statesmen envisioned.

They knew, as we have seen, that fortune had put into their hands a glorious opportunity. They knew that the new nation would have to have a strong government, but they knew also the grave dangers inherent in government when there are no adequate devices to restrain the abuse of that strength. Chance gave them the solution. They created a union of sovereign republics—the 13 states—each possessing in its own right the power to govern its own people within its borders. The Founders built around these states our great central republic. To this the states committed certain powers, clearly defined and thoroughly understood for 148 years. These powers were sharply enumerated in a written constitution. And they were as sharply defined to prevent their extension or enlargement. They proved adequate for 148 years to bring to full growth the freest society that has ever existed in human history.

But now, aside from the mechanical and architectural construction of the federal government—that is, the provisions for a President, a House and Senate and a system of courts, plus certain guarantees—the Constitution has been radically altered and is now accepted in Washington as a charter under which the politicians can erect and administer a powerful central government that can interfere not only with state governmental affairs, but can engage in any kind of political or economic activity inside any state.

In short, *the first stage of the socialist revolution is complete—the stage which consisted in the dismantling of the Constitution and the erection of a powerful central State capable of organizing a socialist society.*

The next stage, of course, is to continue the policy of confiscatory federal taxation and federal borrowing of vast billions to carry on federal activities to increase employment and give handouts to various powerful minorities of all sorts. Along with this goes the evil institution of militarism and its handmaiden, globalism, as a means of creating jobs—millions of jobs at the cost of endless billions in taxation and borrowing. The well-schooled socialist revolutionary knows that the capitalist society cannot stand up under this load of taxation and debt, that it continues to function at present under the impact of war threats and war engines all over the world. This is all to the good for the intelligent socialist revolutionary because he knows that sooner or later the free enterprise system will crash utterly under this load. There are some shallow and giddy leftists who are infatuated by the theory of endless government borrowing. But no intelligent socialist revolutionary who understands the economic structure of our system is fooled by this. He favors it, but he favors it because he knows that it is the most powerful force for an assault on our system that will crush it in the end.

However, there is one feature of this evil development that is overlooked by many honest reformers in our colleges and many of our intellectualist leaders. I have pointed out that while our socialist revolutionaries were promoting the creation of an all-powerful government at the center—powerful enough to operate a socialist society—they were overlooking the ultimate disaster into which they would stumble.

The dream of those who were foremost in promoting the coming of the all-powerful central State and the rise of a noble, free socialist heaven must inevitably run afoul of a law—a law which controls the nature of men. In another section of this discussion I have attempted to describe one of the most pathetic and disturbing aspects of this strange illusion. I have referred to that element in any society which thinks of itself as an intellectual élite. The breed has flourished in every age, and in none more profusely than our own. The reader will recall the earlier pages in which I attempted to describe the weird adventures of the "philosopher rulers" or "philosopher kings" in Bacon's "Salomon's House"; the Communist heaven in Andreae's Christian-apolis; Cabet's dictatorship of the technicians and that zaniest of all the walled heavens right here on our own shores—the Fourierist paradise at Brook Farm in Massachusetts. This experiment excited the imagination of a large collection of teachers, scientists, novelists, poets, essayists and editors, including one famous newspaper editor who became the candidate of a great party for President of the United States.

The era of the little enclosed Communist heavens passed, of course, with the coming of the era of railroads, machines and electric power. The ruthless enterprise of Marx has succeeded the bland visions of Plato and Fourier. But the old illusion hangs on—that these planned socialist societies will be ruled by a breed sometimes called the Technicians and sometimes referred to in various terms that are intended to define the Thinkers, the Philosophers. The intention is differently phrased to suit the fancy of various audiences. Stuart Chase, a kindly and gentle soul, suggests that in this radiant dawn "at the control switches of the nation will stand 100,000 technicians." It is a fair assumption that by this he was not speaking of only one batch of scientific experts. He envisioned the material economic system of a great nation as a number of separate engines of mechanical or economic or social power, all working under the touch of social engineers who would keep the whole economic and political system under their power

—the men of science, the political philosophers, the economic doctors who would make the plans and direct the movements of the production and governing machinery of a vast nation.

There are others who would not agree wholly with this description. They would, perhaps, object to the term "technicians." They would think of America as a vast orderly land of abundance, operating everywhere according to plans laid down by the engineers, the philosophers, the teachers, the thinkers. In other words, we would have in America a great society—a kind of social brotherhood—living in peace, abundance and progress under the guidance, not of a small group in "Salomon's House" but of a class exercising by some political magic a preponderant authority in the management of this broad continent. These are the general outlines of the dream. The details, I assume, will be filled in later, but I suggest we can conclude that the details will be filled in by some pretty harsh, pragmatic gentlemen who will also arrange that the ruthless machine in which the people will be only so many moving parts will be controlled by switches pulled by some American editions of Hitler, Mussolini, Lenin, Stalin and Bulganin. All those kindly, radiant poets and essayists and philosophers in Russia who dreamed so many rosy dreams in the days of the Czars have long since been exterminated out of the machine.

In the United States our cities and states are controlled by professional politicians, often by some who are little seen or heard. Of course an occasional businessman may have an extra added talent for political action, as may also be true of a stray professor—the faculty politician is by no means a rarity. But I suggest we may assume that if a socialist or communist party should ever come to power, it will be run, not by professors, poets, novelists and other scribblers, but by practical politicians who know how to wield and hold power when they get possession of its machinery. The operation of this law is nowhere more pragmatically illustrated than in Soviet Russia. Of the 32 men who sparked and ran the revolution, only two—Stalin and Lenin—continued in power. The other 30 were liquidated. This startling fact has been stated many times, but nowhere more dramatically than in the *Encyclopedia of World Politics* in 1950:

> "Apart from Stalin, few of the old leaders are still in office or indeed alive. Various observers are inclined to describe the Soviet Union as a new class state, in which the bureaucracy has become the ruler class and behaves essentially as the former ruling classes did, even if the political formulas have changed. They believe this new governing class is bent on the consolidation and extension of its power rather than on the old ideals of communism. Nationalism and imperialism in Soviet external policy are added to the symptoms mentioned before to illustrate the critics' thesis that something fundamentally different from the idealistic, internationalist, and egalitarian society of Lenin's dreams has grown in Russia. This school of thought holds that Russia's policy is, generally speaking, determined by national rather than ideological considerations and is using Communists in other countries merely as auxiliaries." [33]

[33] Walter Theimer, *An Encyclopedia of World Politics*, New York, Rinehart & Co., 1950, p. 604.

Russian Communists deny this, but it is a fact. Trotsky, the top partner of Lenin, broke with Stalin on his theory of revolution: that it led to bureaucracy with a primarily nationalist outlook in place of Lenin's dream of an internationalist world. Stalin had become merely the head of a new ruling class and all who questioned this theory were liquidated.

The old socialists in America saw in the launching of the Russian revolution the first radiant chapter in the realization of the socialist dream. But it has brought nothing but frustration and disillusionment. I have a long acquaintance with old socialists in America and it would be very easy to run off a sizable list of able and eminent men who had been caught in the bright dream of a socialist world of peace, freedom and abundance who, in the presence of the bloody reality, have abandoned it. I have given so much space to the role of the intellectual and the so-called intellectual in our own country because it is a fairly new phenomenon here, though it is old in history.

The greatest damage these people effect is to give a glow of intellectual respectability to this dangerous philosophy. And in our own country, where the college has drawn under its influence so large a field of young minds to work on, the campus intellectual enjoys a peculiarly favorable opportunity for sowing in the minds of our youth these baleful doctrines. It is not new. It flourished extensively in the universities of every country in Europe before World War I. And it flourishes on a far more disturbing scale in America now, when college classrooms are so numerous, and when student bodies grow by leaps and bounds and are asked to look at the grave problems of a civilization badly damaged by warmakers and revolutionists of the world. I lay stress on this influence now because the great army of frustrated teachers, writers, lecturers and artists forms one of those minority forces which play an important and effective role not merely in poisoning the minds of our growing generations, but in giving a high degree of respectability to these dangerous ideas. The impact of the socialist philosophy on the mind of a student in Harvard, Columbia, Princeton or Vassar will be very much greater than when it is delivered from a soapbox in Union Square.

The role of the intellectual is as old as history. Robert Hunter, in his brilliant volume *Revolution,* draws a dramatic picture of these intellectual germ carriers in other times:

> "I am at a loss to know how to classify some of the groups of social revolutionists which were to be met with in Paris and other centers of Europe in pre-war days. They were random wantons out of tune with their time but there is something symptomatic of disorders to come in the gathering of the elegants 'of fragrant ringlets, of fashionable mustachios and ruffles . . . of no mean descent and unusual abilities, who only waited the signal to fall like a gang of robbers upon civil society . . .' Thus Mommsen describes a variety of revolutionists in Rome on the eve of Cataline's insurrection. The Comte de Ségur has left us a picture of the same class in Paris before the French revolution: '. . . without regret for the past, without misgiving for the future, we trod gaily on a carpet of flowers which hid the abyss beneath us. . . . All that was antique seemed to us tiresome and ridiculous. . . .

> There is a pleasure in descending so long as one is
> certain of being able to rise again whenever one
> wants to do so . . . *we enjoyed at one and the
> same time the advantages of a patrician status and
> the amenities of a plebeian philosophy.'"* (Italics
> added.)[34]

The picture Hunter draws of Rome before Cata-
line, and of France before Robespierre and before
World War I is nothing less than frightening. He de-
scribes how on occasion when he went to the salons of
these "advocates of ferocious physical vigor," he was
surprised to find around Lagardelle and Sorel "a gentle
and cultured group of ladies and gentlemen, fashion-
ably dressed and luxury loving." He suggests that the
hidden maladies afflicting these people could be diag-
nosed only by a Freud.

Something like this, though by no means so ferocious, can be found in the successors of the Paris salons
right here in our large American cities—particularly
New York and Washington. Intellectualism has become
a kind of fad. It is smart to be at least a little pink. One
is sure of entrée to the best society if one is reasonably
red—that is, can discourse on revolutionary philosophy
but with a Boston accent or even a cultivated North
Carolina drawl. This, I say, is the fashion. Educated or
fashionable people who oppose it gather in small numbers in quiet cocktail parties and try to jest with tolerance of their own futility. What I am trying to say is
that revolution—or socialism, even communism, collec-
tivisms of various types providing the dye is pink or red,

[34] Robert Hunter, *Revolution—Why, How, When?* New York,
Harper, 1940, p. 8.

are now the prevailing mode in the intellectual or fashionable circles. I lay great stress on this because this peculiar province of the revolutionary world plays a powerful role in giving respectability and even money aids to the authentic revolutionary councils, societies, leagues and committees who do the dirty work in the field.

What is written in these pages is wasted unless I have made clear a few simple truths. One is that this country has passed through a series of great and revolutionary changes in its political and economic structure. The American government today and its economic system is radically different from the Republic and the economic system which existed in this country for almost a century and a half. This means nothing less than that we have gone through a political and economic revolution. The changes are not such as are visible to a person strolling along our streets or even to one reading our newspapers. These changes are in the internal organism of our political and economic systems. The object of these changes has been to torture and even ignore the constitutional charter on which our society rests. This was done for the purpose of creating an atmosphere hospitable to the organization and management of a socialist America—but avoiding cautiously the use of the socialist label. It was made possible by a kind of political thuggery by which the sitting justices were driven from the Supreme Court to make room for a benchful of revolutionary judges, or at least compliant political judges, who, in a series of decisions, tortured and twisted the words of the American Constitution to provide a spurious legal atmosphere in which this movement could be carried out.

When our government succeeded in taking us into World War II by a base stratagem it was then quickly equipped with the funds to end the depression by creating a vast war industry—millions of men in the camps and twice or three times as many in the war plants—all financed by confiscatory taxes and huge loans.

But the war is at an end. There is, at least as I write, no fighting anywhere. But the cost of government is still near the war top and the appalling debt hangs over us. Unhappily for all of us, the chickens begin to come home to roost. The President and the New Deal politicians of both parties are confronted with the difficult task of finding an enemy which will serve them instead of war. Russia, of course, serves in a way, but there cannot be any doubt that the gang in the Kremlin enjoys many a grisly jest as it looks over the seas at America in the desperate struggle to find a substitute for war. There is none. And even so, what would it bring? What did we get out of the last one? Russia, with our aid and consent, got two-thirds of Europe and Asia. We got nothing but an empty thing called "Victory," plus a debt of *275 billion dollars, 407,000 boys dead, 670,000 wounded,* and our economic system twisted and deformed and sinking under the weight of our sacrifices and blunders into the arms of the collectivist world.

All this has been made possible by the operation performed by bold politicians and lawless judges on our great federal Republic. The socialist economic system cannot possibly be constructed and operated under our Constitution and within the framework of our federal Republic. To make the collectivist revolution in America possible it was necessary to change the nature of our government. I repeat once more that the first stage in bringing socialism to America was carried through by the socialist revolutionaries and their allies on the packed Supreme Court. Once that was accomplished no legal barrier existed to the formation of a collectivist society in the United States. There is not in either party any energy or sufficient vigor to make any resistance to this evil drift. At the moment, the war hangover, the policy of spending billions in America to produce and supply free all sorts of goods to so-called allies all over the world and to boondoggling minorities all over America keeps the economic system unsteadily afloat. But each new million dollars added to the debt and each new million dug out of the people by taxes brings the nation along with ever-quickening steps toward the precipice. When will it reach the outer limit of this mad policy?

No man can say where the fatal boundary is. But it is somewhere down the road on which we travel—and we move toward it with giant strides. Whether the crisis will come next month or next year it is not possible for any man with only human foresight to predict. But of this we may be sure—that crisis lies somewhere *down the road.*

When that line is reached, then will come the moment of fate for America. Will we sink down helplessly and hopelessly into the arms of the collectivist world? Or will our people rebuild the great Republic of Washington and Jefferson and Madison and Lincoln which for a century and a half was a shining light to enslaved people all over the world?

We must never blind ourselves to this one great idea—that our aim must be not a negative one, not a mere drive *against* the evils that plague us. These evils are the fruit of an alliance of revolutionary sappers and wreckers, ambitious or shortsighted politicians, and various groups seeking purely minority aims. Whatever the aim of any group, the end is the destruction of the American ideal of social organization and of the great Republic built on that ideal. We must be not merely against the destructive programs that beset us. We must be FOR AN IDEAL. We must be dedicated to the rebuilding of the great Republic of our fathers, so shockingly damaged by a dark alliance of communists, socialists, boondogglers, globalists, and certain short-sighted business leaders who for a brief moment float on the surface of the war boom.

But we must be clear as to the nature and shape of that great Republic, which here, as I began, I restate. The goals of civilized society are freedom and security. These ends call for a State capable of ensuring both. The State can ensure freedom. As to security—that is, economic security—it can provide the climate in which men can seek their own security. To do this, the State must erect a government which is the authority by which the society is controlled. Government is an apparatus of power. As such it can become an instrument for the oppression of the citizens in the hands of that body which operates it—the Administration. But the Administration itself, which is actually a collection of individuals generally described as politicians, will be in possession of this apparatus, this government. Once an Administration gets possession of such immense authority, it can be employed to keep the Administration in office and to exploit and even enslave the people. Therefore, the citizens having established government, it is essential that they make some provision for curbing the encroachments of the Administration. They cannot do this merely by the ceremony of election, because at the moment of election the men who hold and wield all the reins of government will be able to buy one group with favors, another with money, while intimidating still others through the vast powers they possess.

This problem was solved in America. The immense energies of government were divided among 48 small republics and one great overall republic. The authority of each was clearly defined and the means of enforcement provided. In short, the State and its terrifying engine of power—government—was brought under control by a written constitution and the division of that power into many different hands, so that no single group of ambitious men could get possession of it all. To ensure the preservation of this system, a judicial system was set up with the ability to restrain any administrative agency from the assumption of powers not entrusted to it.

If I have succeeded in making this clear, the reader will be able to see the revolutionary operation that has been performed on this system by a conspiracy between corrupt and ambitious politicians and a Supreme Court especially packed by a bold stratagem to legalize the assault.

However, the bold aim of the men who have organized and promoted this program is not yet complete, though it has advanced far enough in its aims to make retreat difficult. It must be remembered always that whatever power exists in government, the men who stand at the control switches are not the philosophers and technicians, or intellectuals of any type. They are and always will be politicians, by which I mean men who are ambitious to hold office, who understand the means by which it is acquired and how it can be used to perpetuate their rule. When the political leaders who seek control have in their hands, in addition to those highly limited powers allotted by the Constitution, a whole collection of powers hitherto reserved to the states, their capacity for misrule is greatly increased. But when in addition to this great federal and state political authority, they have also possession of the vast economic agencies and instrumentalities of the nation, they will have a power that the citizens cannot resist.

Let it never be forgotten that this power, however great or small, will always be in the hands of men who are eager for it and who know how to use it to retain their rule. And the greater the collection of powers in their hands, the greater will be their ability to resist ambitious rivals and to silence critical enemies. To all of which let me add one other warning. The men who operate the socialist State—the State that possesses the combined powers of government and industrial and commercial authority with unlimited power to tax—will not be the intellectuals. Neither the philosophers nor the scientists nor the technicians will stand "at the control switches of the nation." It will be the Hitlers, the Mussolinis, the Stalins, the Bulganins, the Perons and their breed.

Chapter XVII

TO

REBUILD

THE

REPUBLIC

I have attempted to outline that series of forces which have involved our country in a frightening series of dangers. It would be difficult to put one's finger on a social disease worse than war itself. Yet, costly as World War II has been for us, the tragic consequences have been even worse than the war. If, in the Second World War, we destroyed the Nazi government of Hitler and the Fascist government of Mussolini, we have performed an operation no less destructive upon our own great constitutional Republic.

As a result of the war we won, we have taken a long step backward. This step may be defined as the dismantling of our Constitution, the altering of the fundamental and essential character of our Republic and the drive to push this great, free nation down the dark and dismal road of collectivism in one of its forms. As we view the future from here, it is perfectly obvious that the victor in this violent and disorderly military and social upheaval is neither of our two political parties, but the socialist movement in the United States.

I have labored in these pages to make it clear that it is impossible to organize and operate a socialist society in the United States under the American Constitution. That Constitution recognized and sought to erect a system of government in which the vast and dread power of government would be committed not to one central State, but to a number of separate sovereign agencies—the federal government and the 48 states. And even these powers were strictly limited, not only in the states themselves but, on a far more severe scale, in the federal government. I repeat that here was power —political power—provided on a great scale, but so ordered that no single administration could take into its hands all of the dread authority of government. Furthermore, the greatest caution was taken to prevent any alteration of this important device save by formal amendment of the Constitution. This arrangement, hailed all over the world, remained essentially in its original form until 1933—a period of 144 years.

The tragic transformation of this civilized system, however, has been accomplished without any legal authority and without the American people being aware of the disaster that has overtaken them. The depression of 1929, which was the work of certain lawless elements in our business world, was in no sense due to the government itself or the system of government. That depression had actually spread not only over America but all over Europe under many different government forms. It was, so far as America was concerned, a crime —a crime perpetrated on our society by a group of economic desperadoes in our business world. But the repercussions resulted in creating an atmosphere in which another group of outlaws—political adventurers—were able to assault and wreck the great structure of the American Republic. The mere outlines remain, but the unique and essential elements that gave it vitality are almost gone. A dark alliance among a horde of corrupt politicians, shallow businessmen, a packed Supreme Court and a coalition of socialist and communist revolutionaries has almost completed this evil task.

The result is the erection of a central government which, without any constitutional base, has usurped the authority to carry on the functions of government not only within the federal area staked out by the Constitution, but within the states as well. But, far more serious, it has asserted and used on an immense scale the authority to enter the field of enterprise, to organize and operate practically every kind of business adventure. In other words, the federal government, under the administrations of both political parties, has now definitely been committed not merely to the administration of political power within its constitutional limits, but in the states themselves and, in addition, to the organization and management of business enterprise. We are, as a matter of fact, now more than knee deep in a socialist society. The only question that confronts us is: Will we go forward to complete this infamy or will we return to the Republic of the Constitution?

One of the most terrifying aspects of this whole episode in our history is the fact that, trapped in a dismal failure to produce prosperity, our government turned to the oldest and most tragic boondoggle of history—war. By means of the war and the post-war mess, our government has managed to keep an evil prosperity going, based on continuous confiscatory taxes, endless borrowing, fantastic adventures abroad, a crooked pretense of war on the Soviet which we saved with our military aid and perpetuated with our Treasury, and which we now nurse as an enemy—not because we fear her clumsy system in a military sense but because we need her. We need her as the enemy this corrupt system requires to keep the taxes and the borrowing and the spending going.

There is something tragic in the confident boast of our little rulers in Washington that they have given us a robust prosperity and will continue to do so. There is no doubt we have had employment on an extraordinary scale, with an accompanying huge national income. But by what dangerous means has this "miracle" been worked?

When the European war began in 1939, Mr. Roosevelt had been in office for 6½ years and had not, as we have seen, brought prosperity to this country. There were 44,993,000 people employed, but there were still 11,369,000 unemployed. Then came the war and by the time it ended in 1945 we had 61,653,000 employed. This represented an increase in employment of 16,660,-000 people. This is easily explained. A vast horde of men—and some women—were called into the armed services. In 1929 there were only 255,233 men in the armed services. But when the war got under way, we began with 9,044,000 in the services in 1942, and by 1945 we had 12,123,000. Thus in those years we employed from 9 to over 12 million in the armed forces. But besides that, far more were employed in the munitions plants, the shipyards, the steel, iron and other plants manufacturing weapons, planes, tanks, etc. Unemployment was more than wiped out by war and paid for with confiscatory taxes and incredible mountains of borrowed funds—*over 250 billion dollars*—still due and growing every year since. Today the interest on the debt alone is well over *6 billion dollars,* or twice the total cost of the federal government when Roosevelt took office.

There is one other illustration that will aid the reader in understanding the enormity of the policy by which this fraudulent prosperity has been created. In 1954, the total cost of the federal government was $67,-772,000,000. How was it spent?:

On armaments	$46,522,000,000
On international affairs	1,553,000,000
On veterans' services	4,249,000,000
On interest on the debt	6,382,000,000
TOTAL	58,706,000,000

Thus, on the ordinary functions of government, the federal administration spent $9,066,000,000, but $58,-700,000,000 on armaments, international and veterans' affairs and interest on the war debt—and this, 9 years after World War II had ended.

There is a school of radical economists and social doctrinaires highly placed in Washington whose theories follow closely those which dominated the Roosevelt and Truman administrations. They hold that public debt need not be feared and that it is the most powerful fertilizer of the national economy. It is true that borrowing by either government or business can, within rational limits, be used with great and salutary effects. But no sane man can defend the principle of endless borrowing, taxation and spending to produce prosperity. There is a promise from Washington that the budget will be balanced in 1956. This, however, is a mere sleight-of-hand performance. The promise is based on the hope of the government to borrow so much in 1955 that it will have some surplus with which to operate in 1956.

The debt, as we have seen, has been rising steadily. It was 266 billion in 1952. It is 278 billion as of April, 1955—an increase of *12 billion dollars*. At present the interest charge on this is close to 7 billion dollars. But the interest rate is constantly rising. This means that it will not be long before a great deal of the short-term, low-interest bonds will be maturing and must be refunded at higher rates. The total interest charge, sooner or later, will be not less than *9 or 10 billion dollars*. It is difficult for those of us who are not accustomed to deal with such fantastic sums to realize the gravity of this fact. Perhaps we will be able to grasp it if we recall that the entire cost of operating the national government and all the state, county and municipal governments in the United States before Roosevelt did not exceed by very much this huge sum.

Let no one comfort his soul with the fatuous hope that we can keep this wicked half-war going or that we can keep this dangerous boom afloat on the evil system of militarism which, like most of the balance of our New Deal, we have copied from the bedeviled politicians of Europe. Yet this is precisely what our government seeks to attempt in search of an enterprise on which to spend continuous floods of taxes and borrowed money. The President has already declared his desire to establish here the system of Universal Military Training, which he borrows from the wrecked and bankrupt pre-war governments of Germany, Italy, Austria, France and other European countries. The President, perhaps, does not know that militarism in those countries was not a mere pet institution of the military caste. It could never have been established in any of these countries but for the immense economic effects it produced—taking millions of men out of the labor market and providing them with uniforms, food, barracks and weapons, all paid for by the governments out of confiscatory taxes and crushing debts. The end of it for all of them was approaching bankruptcy. And from this they sought escape in the war of 1914.

To the intolerable and growing interest charge on the debt, the President now seeks to add the further burden of permanent militarism as a substitute for war —which will mean endless additions to the national debt until we sink down in some grave and terrifying economic catastrophe. Every country in Europe that turned to this evil institution did it for precisely the reasons that move the President. But, by 1914, every country that adopted it, along with welfare and social services and various socialistic experiments, was on the verge of bankruptcy and turned in desperation to outright war as an escape. For America, too, there is a day of reckoning ahead. It is to alert the American people to that moment that I have written this book.

Of course the politicians interested in public money and our noisy and treacherous Leftists will ask: Do you want to go back? Of course not. We want to go forward. But we have reached a road block in our civilization and have wandered off on a fork in the road. We have been stumbling under the guidance of hot-headed socialist revolutionaries and corrupt politicians into a wilderness. *We must go back in order to go forward. We must return to the great highway of the American Republic.*

Obviously the nation faces a tremendous reconstruction job on our mutilated Constitution and on our sadly battered Republic. Whatever we do, this must stand first in the order of reconstruction—to restore to its historic shape and dimensions the Constitution of the United States. We must redefine its purpose—to chart a government for an assemblage of free republics, not to assume the role of guide, repairman, financier and policeman of any other part of the world. The exception to this, of course, would be our adherence to the Monroe Doctrine, to keep the imperialist nations of the Old World out of this hemisphere. Our objectives must have for their essential features the following proposals.

A

The first and most challenging enterprise is to return the federal Constitution to its historic limits as construed by the Supreme Court for 145 years. No proof is necessary of the bold design of President Roosevelt, guided by the audacious crew of socialist and communist revolutionaries who surrounded him. That design was to alter the Constitution by judicial interpretation. The amendment of the Constitution can be legally effected by only one method—and that is set out in the instrument itself. Unable to carry out this revolutionary alteration of the government by lawful methods, Roosevelt turned to an outrageous assault upon the judges of the Supreme Court for the purpose of driving them off the bench and replacing them with compliant political judges—some of them social revolutionists—who could be depended on to torture the words of the Constitution into such meanings as would literally alter the whole shape and nature of our federal system. This assault was made possible by the lawless mind of the President, the boldness of the conspirators who surrounded him, and the disturbed and troubled state of the public mind under the influence of the depression.

The escape from the consequences of this great crime against our society is perhaps the most difficult of all the problems that confront us. The infamy which characterizes this adventure, however, justifies a bold counterstroke to correct it. But it is a stroke that can be carried out within the clear meaning of the Constitution. I urge a constitutional amendment, and suggest the following wording:

> The decisions of the Supreme Court between 1937 and the date of the final adoption of this amendment, rendered by a Court designedly packed to alter by interpretation the clear meanings of the Constitution, are hereby declared to have no force and effect as precedents in judicial or other proceedings in determining the meaning of the words, sections and provisions of the Constitution of the United States.

B

Next in order should come a complete repudiation of the United Nations and the removal of that organization, if continued by other countries, from this hemisphere.

C

The repeal of the 16th Amendment (the Income Tax Amendment) to the Constitution should hold a high place in this great project of reconstruction. The men who proposed the adoption of that measure never envisioned the shocking abuses that would be fostered and legalized under it. As of this moment the nation stands on the verge of bankruptcy because of this amendment, which was not effected until after more than a hundred years of the Republic and then by men who never dreamed it would be subjected to such incredible abuses. I suggest an outright repeal of the 16th Amendment. It is at the root of almost every abuse which has brought this nation into so much distress and involved us in difficulties all over the world.

D

Next in order should be the adoption of what is known as the Bridges-Byrd Amendment to the Constitution to protect the people, their institutions and their liberties from the outrageous abuses of power in the hands of a federal administration armed not only with the immense power to tax without limit, but to borrow without limit. It is this dangerous weapon that has been used to bring the government to the brink of bankruptcy.

Senator Styles Bridges and Senator Harry Byrd, both eminent leaders in their respective parties, have proposed an amendment aimed at ending this great abuse. It would prohibit the federal government, except in time of actual, declared warfare, from spending more than it can collect in taxes. In other words, the federal government would be required to pay as it goes and to put an end definitely to the destructive policy begun by President Roosevelt of borrowing and borrowing and spending and spending. This amendment should stand high in the proposals of any political or social group interested in the restoration of the American system of organized life and the protection of the people from lawless central government.

E

For 20 years the federal government has, by every devious device, attempted to evade and defy the plain provisions of the Constitution limiting its powers. Now a new proposal has been offered by President Eisenhower to evade the clear limitations imposed by law on the borrowing power, the taxing power, and the executive authority of the government by creating a corporation. It would resemble any other business corporation, and could borrow funds on the faith of its own credit and engage in activities within the states utterly outside the constitutional functions of the federal government. It would not have to go to Congress for funds, but would raise them by the issuance of its own bonds and would finance its operation by the collection of taxes and tolls in its own name. The federal government would be a mere stockholder in this giant octopus. If the federal government can do this to build roads inside the states, wholly outside its constitutional authority, it can do anything.

The fact that such a bold and preposterous proposal should come from the President of the United States is a clear evidence of the fact that there is in this country a cabal whose intention is to wipe out our federal system and slowly reduce our Constitution to a mere shadow.

A constitutional amendment should be adopted without delay asserting that no bureau or department or corporation in which the federal government holds any part of the shares can perform any act which the government itself is forbidden to perform in its own name.

F

Another proposal essential to the safety of the American Republic is known as the Bricker Amendment, pending, as I write, before the United States Senate. Recently a strangely bold assertion of power in the Executive has been put forward, the purpose of which is to enable the Executive to bypass the Congress and the Constitution in the imposition of laws and regulations on the American people by means of a treaty. The claim is made that the Executive can enter into a treaty with a foreign power which, if approved by the Senate alone, can become effective as law in the United States even though it conflicts clearly with the Constitution; this means that it can become effective as internal law even if it conflicts with the Bill of Rights.

Senator John Bricker of Ohio has proposed an amendment to the Constitution to put an end to this outrageous claim. There have been several versions of this amendment, but its essential clauses are as follows:

1. A provision of a treaty or other international agreement which conflicts with this Constitution, or which is not made in pursuance thereof, shall not be the supreme law of the land nor be of any force or effect.
2. A treaty or other international agreement shall become effective as internal law in the United States only through legislation valid in the absence of international agreement.

Let no fearful soul declare that these great and essential measures cannot be passed. This is the counsel of timidity. One virtue, at least, we ought to copy from our enemies and the enemies of the Republic. The incredible work of distortion and disruption and bankruptcy and endless global dangers was imposed on our government by a very small clique of revolutionary conspirators, most of whom were utterly unknown and without any political influence when this evil enterprise began. They represented minorities and in some cases small minorities—but minorities ablaze with conviction and resolution. The proposals suggested here have, beyond all doubt, the support of vast and overwhelming numbers of the American people. All that is lacking is leadership.

In the last 25 years we have seen all the advances in human freedom, won through so many centuries though in different degrees, wiped out in Europe in what might be called a great retreat from freedom. Now we see the initial steps in that retreat here in the United

States of America. Americans have a great ideal *to be for*. That ideal is not to restore freedom to Europe, which is all through with the quest for freedom, or to support socialist regimes all over the world. Our ideal must be to rebuild our own great Republic in America.

APPENDIX

On the seventh day of June, 1776, in the assembly chamber of the State House in Philadelphia, the Continental Congress of the United Colonies was in session. The long quarrel between George III and his American subjects had reached its climax. We need not repeat here the details of that quarrel about a long list of grievances affecting trade, taxes, invasions of legislative rights, imposition of controlled judges, military abuses and other crimes against the liberties of the people.

Two years had passed since this Congress had first met. It had not convened then to make war on England, which its members looked on as their mother country. They wished merely to combine their strength to force those reforms which a foolish monarch and his compliant ministers would not grant willingly.

But actual warfare had broken out. The battle of

173

Lexington had been fought. Ticonderoga, Bunker Hill, Quebec, the evacuation of Boston, a whole train of events gave to the situation but one meaning, that these colonies were at war.

Nevertheless they still clung to the hope that the king would listen to reason. They sent a delegate to London to present a last appeal for justice and kindness from the British government. The king refused even to receive him.

Blood had been shed. An American army was in the field under command of Washington. North Carolina had declared in favor of a separation. Colony after colony followed until all but New York had proclaimed their willingness to make the break.

And now in Philadelphia the representatives of the colonies were in session. On June 7, Richard Henry Lee of Virginia, in a clear voice, read a resolution:

> "That these united colonies are, and of right
> ought to be, free and independent states; that they
> are absolved from all allegiance to the British
> crown; and that all political connection between
> them and the State of Great Britain is, and ought
> to be, totally dissolved."

John Adams seconded the resolution. It was debated on July 1 and adopted July 2. Meantime a committee had been named to prepare the form which the declaration should take. Its members were Thomas Jefferson, John Adams, Benjamin Franklin, Roger Sherman and Robert Livingston.

Jefferson was made chairman of the committee. He went to work at once to write a statement to be issued to the world in support of the coming break.

Immediately after voting independence of Britain, the Congress took up the report of Jefferson's committee and the resolution which he had drawn. He was, of all men in the colonies, best fitted for the task and the draft read to the Congress was his, subject to only a few minor verbal changes by other members of the committee. After three days' debate, it was adopted on July 4, 1776. In every respect it is the noblest document in the history of the great struggle for human freedom. Its opening phrases remain as a sort of scripture for true liberals the world over:

> "We hold these truths to be self-evident, that all men are created equal, that they are endowed by their Creator with certain unalienable Rights, that among these are Life, Liberty and the pursuit of Happiness. That to secure these rights, Governments are instituted among Men, deriving their just powers from the consent of the governed."

It is these few lines which mark this great instrument as the farthest point yet reached by civilized man as a basis for the government he was about to launch.

These ideas were not new. The philosopher John Locke had maintained that men have natural rights and that governments were instituted with only such specific powers as might be granted them by the governed.

Locke's "Two Treatises on Government," written in 1690, were widely read and well known to the thinking men of America. And it must be remembered that the largest element in America was made up of the spiritual and political descendants of the old Puritans who had once deposed a king.

But in all truth this was a natural step for the Americans. Their fathers already asserted and established the doctrine that authority inheres somewhere among the people and can be invoked to dethrone a king when he imposes on their freedom. They had established the proposition that the people have a right to govern and that the king must rule through ministers which they can approve.

This theory was at the moment in eclipse in England.

But only for the moment. Of course the English had divided the people into classes: the élite, the landowners and the masses. This élite had an equal share with the others, indeed a greater than equal share. And the masses were largely excluded, not irrevocably but subject to the acquisition of property. The Americans were ready for the next step—one of the most momentous in human history.

Some years ago a lady spinner of detective yarns departed from her trade long enough to have a good sneer at the Declaration of Independence. Of course, she observed, all men are not equal. That is too obvious. Look at them—tall and short, strong and weak, intelligent and stupid, industrious and lazy.

It did not occur to her that such observant men as old Ben Franklin, and Thomas Jefferson had not failed to note these differences. The meaning of the Declaration is clear—all men are created *equal before the law*—they have the same right to life, liberty and the pursuit of happiness, and governments must get their powers from them. That is the rock on which American freedom is built.

Seven years of war, sacrifice and valor made the American colonies free of England. After seven more years of dissension and civil strife, it was now clear the colonists must set up a government for themselves that would assure them the freedoms they had proclaimed and fought for. On May 14, 1787, delegates from all the states met in Philadelphia in convention. When, four months later, they had finished their task they had, as Gladstone phrased it, produced "the most wonderful work ever struck at a given time by the brain and purpose of man."

If ever an American can feel in any shrine the living presence of the venerated dead, it is in the chamber of that building in Philadelphia where the Declaration of Independence was adopted and where the Constitution of the United States was framed.

It has seemed to many that there must have been some divine intervention in an arrangement that brought together so many extraordinary men in so critical a moment of history. One may, without any false emotion, admit that he stands in awe of the grandeur of the edifice which they reared.

It is said that as the convention adjourned the members themselves were suddenly touched with a sense of awe at what they had done. Washington sat with bowed head in the President's chair.

The aged Franklin, amidst the prevailing silence, rose. A half sun with its gilded rays was carved on the back of the chair occupied by George Washington. Franklin said: "As I have been sitting here all these weeks, I have often wondered whether yonder sun is rising or setting. But now I know that it is a rising sun." As Franklin, with others, left the building, someone in the crowd outside asked him what kind of government they had set up. He replied: "A republic—if we can keep it so."

However, we must be careful not to ascribe to these great men more than is just. They did not invent all the parts of this system. Thirteen hundred years of English history looked down on them and they knew that history. They knew of those institutions and laws which, through the centuries, had been forged by their fathers in blood and suffering.

They proposed to build a government upon the theory that man had a right to be free and that the chief purpose of government was to protect him in that freedom. They did not think they were organizing a super-welfare agency which would act as guide, philosopher, planning agency, loan broker and moral policeman of the common man.

As the center of their system they took the mighty instrument of parliamentary government. They built on that.

They knew the reliance their fathers had placed upon law—law settled and explicit, founded in the mores and consent of the people—law rather than the good will of a prince or some supposedly benevolent autocrat.

They knew well that power can corrupt a good man and make a devil of a bad one. And they knew that, in government as at a barn dance, he who pays the piper calls the tune, and that the most powerful weapon in the hands of a free people is the secure possession of the purse strings.

They knew that the chief weakness in every government ever set up anywhere was the executive and that nothing had yet been found to prevent an executive from working incessantly to extend his power.

They determined to limit the powers of government, to give it no more powers than were necessary to ensure the safety and freedom of the people—freedom from an external enemy, freedom from rapacious and aggressive individuals *and freedom from the government itself.*

I have said this structure was not wholly new. By that I mean that many of its component parts were old and tried. But it is not true to say that the government setup in Philadelphia was a modified form of the British system. It was a distinctly new kind of government. What they established may well be called the American system.

Their plan was simple. In fact the conditions of the country's existing institutions providentially made it almost mandatory. It began with the assumption that all sovereignty resided in the people. Out of this sovereignty the people would give to the government only such powers as were essential to its great objective. However, it would not entrust these powers to any one agency.

The great bulk of governmental power would be localized in the several communities—the states—each to govern its people in accordance with their differing tastes and conditions. The central or federal government would have only such powers as were needed for dealing with foreign nations, national defense, the currency and the control of such matters as were interstate in nature and were the common concern of all the states.

But to be sure that this central government, which rightly was the agency that all feared, could not build itself into a despotism, the functions of this government were divided among three separate and independent functionaries —the Congress to make the laws, the President to administer them with a supervisory interest in the law-making, and a Judicial system to interpret the laws.

The founders of this system understood that there would be occasions when such a government might find itself a little clumsy. This they preferred to the danger of the government having too much power, including the power to oppress their fellow men.

But, unlike any other government that ever existed, the founders withheld from all of these agencies certain great powers of government *which were retained in the hands of the people.*

Beyond a doubt no government that has ever existed was ever so well designed to achieve the purpose in the minds of its builders—namely the protection of the freedom of its citizens. It was not designed to manage the citizen's affairs, to be his partner in business, to be his banker, his doctor, his lawyer, his economic counsellor.

It was designed to be the protector of his freedom. And in no other land in history has man enjoyed such wide freedom as in the country which has lived under this beneficent system. This, the American Constitution, was the greatest charter of all.

As it is impossible to understand or discuss the American Republic without a clear understanding of the Constitution itself, the full text of that instrument, with all of its amendments, is printed here.

THE

CONSTITUTION

OF THE

UNITED

STATES

We the People of the United States, in Order to form a more perfect Union, establish Justice, insure domestic Tranquility, provide for the common defense, promote the general Welfare, and secure the Blessings of Liberty to ourselves and our Posterity, do ordain and establish this Constitution for the United States of America.

ARTICLE I

Section 1. All legislative Powers herein granted shall be vested in a Congress of the United States, which shall consist of a Senate and House of Representatives.

Section 2. The House of Representatives shall be composed of Members chosen every second Year by the People of the several States, and the Electors in each State shall have the Qualifications requisite for Electors of the most numerous Branch of the State Legislature.

No Person shall be a Representative who shall not have attained to the Age of twenty five Years, and been seven Years a Citizen of the United States, and who shall not, when elected, be an Inhabitant of that State in which he shall be chosen.

Representatives and direct Taxes shall be apportioned among the several States which may be included within this Union, according to their respective Numbers, which shall be determined by adding to the whole Number of free Persons, including those bound to Service for a Term of Years, and excluding Indians not taxed, three fifths of all other Persons. The actual Enumeration shall be made within three Years after the first Meeting of the Congress of the United States, and within every subsequent Term of ten Years, in such Manner as they shall by Law direct. The Number of Representatives shall not exceed one for every thirty Thousand, but each State shall have at Least one 'Representative; and until such enumeration shall be made, the State of New Hampshire shall be entitled to choose three, Massachusetts eight, Rhode-Island and Providence Plantations one, Connecticut five, New-York six, New Jersey four, Pennsylvania eight, Delaware one, Maryland six, Virginia ten, North Carolina five, South Carolina five, and Georgia three.

When vacancies happen in the Representation from any State, the Executive Authority thereof shall issue Writs of Election to fill such Vacancies.

The House of Representatives shall choose their speaker and other Officers; and shall have the sole Power of Impeachment.

Section 3. The Senate of the United States shall be composed of two Senators from each State, chosen by the Legislature thereof, for six Years; and each Senator shall have one Vote.

Immediately after they shall be assembled in Consequence of the first Election, they shall be divided as equally as may be into three Classes. The Seats of the Senators of the first Class shall be vacated at the Expiration of the second Year, of the second Class at the Expiration of the fourth Year, and of the third Class at the Expiration of the sixth Year, so that one third may be chosen every second Year; and if Vacancies happen by Resignation, or otherwise, during the Recess of the Legislature of any State, the Executive thereof may make temporary Appointments until the next Meeting of the Legislature, which shall then fill such Vacancies.

No Person shall be a Senator who shall not have attained to the Age of thirty years, and been nine Years a Citizen of the United States, and who shall not, when elected, be an Inhabitant of that State for which he shall be chosen.

The Vice President of the United States shall be President of the Senate, but shall have no Vote, unless they be equally divided.

The Senate shall choose their other Officers, and also a President pro tempore, in the Absence of the Vice President, or when he shall exercise the Office of President of the United States.

The Senate shall have the sole Power to try all Impeachments. When sitting for that Purpose, they shall be on Oath or Affirmation. When the President of the United States is tried, the Chief Justice shall preside: And no Person shall be convicted without the Concurrence of two thirds of the Members present.

Judgment in Cases of Impeachment shall not extend further than to removal from Office, and disqualification to hold and enjoy any Office of Honor, Trust or Profit under the United States: but the Party convicted shall nevertheless be liable and subject to Indictment, Trial, Judgment and Punishment, according to Law.

Section 4. The Times, Places and Manner of holding Elections for Senators and Representatives, shall be prescribed in each State by the Legislature thereof; but the Congress may at any time by Law make or alter such Regulations, except as to the Places of choosing Senators.

The Congress shall assemble at least once in every Year, and such Meeting shall be on the first Monday in December, unless they shall by Law appoint a different Day.

Section 5. Each House shall be the Judge of the Elections, Returns and Qualifications of its own Members, and a Majority of each shall constitute a Quorum to do Business; but a smaller Number may adjourn from day to day, and may be authorized to compel the Attendance of Absent Members, in such Manner, and under such Penalties as each House may provide.

Each House may determine the Rules of its Proceedings, punish its Members for disorderly Behaviour, and, with the Concurrence of two thirds, expel a Member.

Each House shall keep a Journal of its Proceedings, and from time to time publish the same, excepting such Parts as may in their Judgment require Secrecy; and the Yeas and Nays of the Members of either House on any question shall, at the Desire of one fifth of those Present, be entered on the Journal.

Neither House, during the Session of Congress shall, without the Consent of the other, adjourn for more than three Days, nor to any other Place than that in which the two Houses shall be sitting.

Section 6. The Senators and Representatives shall receive a Compensation for their Services, to be ascertained by Law, and paid out of the Treasury of the United States. They shall in all Cases, except Treason, Felony and Breach of the Peace, be privileged from Arrest during their Attendance at the Session of their respective Houses, and in going to and returning from the same; and for any Speech or Debate in either House, they shall not be questioned in any other Place.

No Senator or Representative shall, during the Time for

which he was elected, be appointed to any civil Office under the Authority of the United States, which shall have been created, or the Emoluments whereof shall have been increased during such Time; and no Person holding any Office under the United States, shall be a Member of either House during his Continuance in Office.

Section 7. All Bills for raising Revenue shall originate in the House of Representatives; but the Senate may purpose or concur with Amendments as on other Bills.

Every Bill which shall have passed the House of Representatives and the Senate shall, before it becomes a Law, be presented to the President of the United States; If he approve he shall sign it, but if not he shall return it, with his Objections to that House in which it shall have originated, who shall enter the Objections at large on their Journal, and proceed to reconsider it. If after such Reconsideration two thirds of that House shall agree to pass the Bill, it shall be sent, together with the Objections, to the other House, by which it shall likewise be reconsidered, and if approved by two thirds of that House, it shall become a Law. But in all such Cases the Votes of both Houses shall be determined by Yeas and Nays, and the Names of the Persons voting for and against the Bill shall be entered on the Journal of each House respectively. If any Bill shall not be returned by the President within ten Days (Sundays excepted) after it shall have been presented to him, the Same shall be a Law, in like Manner as if he had signed it, unless the Congress by their Adjournment prevent its Return, in which Case it shall not be a Law.

Every Order, Resolution, or Vote to which the Concurrence of the Senate and House of Representatives may be necessary (except on a question of Adjournment) shall be presented to the President of the United States; and before the Same shall take Effect, shall be approved by him, or being disapproved by him, shall be repassed by two thirds of the Senate and House of Representatives, according to the Rules and Limitations prescribed in the Case of a Bill.

Section 8. The Congress shall have the Power to lay and collect Taxes, Duties, Imposts and Excises, to pay the Debts and provide for the common Defence and general Welfare of the United States; but all Duties, Imposts and Excises shall be uniform throughout the United States;

To borrow Money on the Credit of the United States;

To regulate Commerce with foreign Nations, and among the several States, and with the Indian Tribes;

To establish an uniform Rule of Naturalization, and uniform Laws on the subject of Bankruptcies throughout the United States;

To coin Money, regulate the Value thereof, and of foreign Coin, and fix the Standard of Weights and Measures;

To provide for the Punishment of counterfeiting the Securities and current Coin of the United States;

To establish Post Offices and Post Roads;

To promote the Progress of Science and useful Arts, by securing for limited Times to Authors and Inventors the exclusive Right to their respective Writings and Discoveries;

To constitute Tribunals inferior to the Supreme Court;

To define and punish Piracies and Felonies committed on the high Seas, and Offences against the Law of Nations;

To declare War, grant Letters of Marque and Reprisal, and make Rules concerning Captures on Land and Water;

To raise and support Armies, but no Appropriation of Money to that Use shall be for a longer Term than two Years;

To provide and maintain a Navy;

To make Rules for the Government and Regulation of the land and naval Forces;

To provide for calling forth the Militia to execute the

Laws of the Union, suppress Insurrections and repel Invasions;

To provide for organizing, arming, and disciplining, the Militia, and for governing such Part of them as may be employed in the Service of the United States, reserving to the States respectively, the Appointment of the Officers, and the Authority of training the Militia according to the Discipline prescribed by Congress;

To exercise exclusive Legislation in all Cases whatsoever, over such District (not exceeding ten Miles square) as may, by Cession of particular States, and the Acceptance of Congress, become the Seat of the Government of the United States, and to exercise like Authority over all Places purchased by the Consent of the Legislature of the State in which the Same shall be for the Erection of Forts, Magazines, Arsenals, dock-Yards, and other needful Buildings;—And

To make all Laws which shall be necessary and proper for carrying into Execution the foregoing Powers, and all other Powers vested by this Constitution in the Government of the United States, or in any Department or Officer thereof.

Section 9. The Migration or Importation of such Persons as any of the States now existing shall think proper to admit, shall not be prohibited by the Congress prior to the Year one thousand eight hundred and eight, but a Tax or duty may be imposed on such Importation, not exceeding ten Dollars for each Person.

The Privilege of the Writ of Habeas Corpus shall not be suspended, unless when in Cases of Rebellion or Invasion the public Safety may require it.

No Bill of Attainder or ex post facto Law shall be passed.

No Capitation, or other direct, Tax shall be laid, unless in Proportion to the Census or Enumeration herein before directed to be taken.

No Tax or Duty shall be laid on Articles exported from any State.

No Preference shall be given by any Regulation of Commerce or Revenue to the Ports of one State over those of another; nor shall Vessels bound to, or from, one State, be obligated to enter, clear, or pay Duties in another.

No Money shall be drawn from the Treasury, but in Consequence of Appropriations made by Law; and a regular Statement and Account of the Receipts and Expenditures of all public Money shall be published from time to time.

No Title of Nobility shall be granted by the United States: And no Person holding any Office of Profit or Trust under them, shall, without the Consent of the Congress, accept of any present, Emolument, Office, or Title, of any kind whatever, from any King, Prince, or foreign State.

Section 10. No State shall enter into any Treaty, Alliance, or Confederation; grant Letters of Marque and Reprisal; coin Money; emit Bills of Credit; make any Thing but gold and silver Coin a Tender in Payment of Debts; pass any Bill of Attainder, ex post facto Law, or Law impairing the Obligation of Contracts, or grant any Title of Nobility.

No State shall, without the Consent of the Congress, lay any Imposts or Duties on Imports or Exports, except what may be absolutely necessary for executing its inspection Laws: and the net Produce of all Duties and Imposts, laid by any State on Imports or Exports, shall be for the Use of the Treasury of the United States; and all such Laws shall be subject to the Revision and Control of the Congress.

No State shall, without the Consent of Congress, lay any Duty of Tonnage, keep Troops, or Ships of War in time of Peace, enter into any Agreement or Compact with another State, or with a foreign Power, or engage in War, unless actually invaded, or in such imminent Danger as will not admit of delay.

ARTICLE II

Section 1. The executive Power shall be vested in a President of the United States of America. He shall hold his Office during the Term of four Years, and, together with the Vice President, chosen for the same Term, be elected, as follows;

Each State shall appoint, in such Manner as the Legislature thereof may direct, a Number of Electors, equal to the whole Number of Senators and Representatives to which the State may be entitled in the Congress: but no Senator or Representative, or Person holding an Office of Trust or Profit under the United States, shall be appointed an Elector.

The Electors shall meet in their respective States, and vote by Ballot for two Persons, of whom one at least shall not be an Inhabitant of the same State with themselves. And they shall make a List of all the Persons voted for, and of the Number of Votes for each; which List they shall sign and certify, and transmit sealed to the Seat of the Government of the United States, directed to the President of the Senate. The President of the Senate shall, in the Presence of the Senate and House of Representatives, open all the Certificates, and the Votes shall then be counted. The Person having the greatest Number of Votes shall be President, if such Number be a Majority of the whole Number of Electors appointed; and if there be more than one who have such Majority, and have an equal Number of Votes, then the House of Representatives shall immediately choose by Ballot one of them for President; and if no Person have a Majority, then from the five highest on the List the said House shall in like Manner choose the President. But in choosing the President, the Votes shall be taken by States, the Representation from each State having one Vote; A Quorum for this Purpose shall consist of a Member or Members from two thirds of the States, and a Majority of all the States shall be necessary to a Choice. In every Case, after the Choice of the President, the Person having the greatest Number of Votes of the Electors shall be the Vice President. But if there should remain two or more who have equal Votes, the Senate shall choose from them by Ballot the Vice President.

The Congress may determine the Time of choosing the Electors, and the Day on which they shall give their Votes; which Day shall be the same throughout the United States.

No Person except a natural born Citizen, or a Citizen of the United States, at the time of the Adoption of this Constitution, shall be eligible to the Office of President; neither shall any Person be eligible to that Office who shall not have attained to the Age of thirty five Years, and been fourteen Years a Resident within the United States.

In Case of the Removal of the President from Office, or of his Death, Resignation, or Inability to discharge the Powers and Duties of the said Office, the Same shall devolve on the Vice President, and the Congress may by Law provide for the Case of Removal, Death, Resignation or Inability, both of the President and Vice President, declaring what Officer shall then act as President, and such Officer shall act accordingly, until the Disability be removed, or a President shall be elected.

The President shall, at stated Times, receive for his Services, a Compensation, which shall neither be encreased nor diminished during the Period for which he shall have been elected, and he shall not receive within that Period any other Emolument from the United States, or any of them.

Before he enter on the Execution of his Office, he shall take the following Oath or Affirmation:—"I do solemnly swear (or affirm) that I will faithfully execute the Office of President of the United States, and will to the best of my Ability, preserve, protect and defend the Constitution of the United States."

Section 2. The President shall be Commander in Chief of the Army and Navy of the United States, and of the Militia of the several States, when called into the actual Service of the United States; he may require the Opinion, in writing, of the principal Officer in each of the executive Departments, upon any Subject relating to the Duties of their respective Offices, and he shall have Power to grant Reprieves and Pardons for Offences against the United States except in Cases of Impeachment.

He shall have Power, by and with the Advice and Consent of the Senate, to make Treaties, provided two thirds of the Senators concur; and he shall nominate, and by and with the Advice and Consent of the Senate, shall appoint Ambassadors, other public Ministers and Consuls, Judges of the supreme Court, and all other Officers of the United States, whose Appointments are not herein otherwise provided for, and which shall be established by Law: but the Congress may by Law vest the Appointment of such inferior Officers, as they think proper, in the President alone, in the Courts of Law, or in the Heads of Departments.

The President shall have Power to fill up all Vacancies that may happen during the Recess of the Senate, by granting Commissions which shall expire at the End of their next Session.

Section 3. He shall from time to time give to the Congress Information of the State of the Union, and recommend to their Consideration such Measures as he shall judge necessary and expedient; he may, on extraordinary Occasions, convene both Houses, or either of them, and in Case of Disagreement between them, with Respect to the Time of Adjournment, he may adjourn them to such Time as he shall think proper; he shall receive Ambassadors and other public Ministers; he shall take Care that the Laws be faithfully executed, and shall Commission all the Officers of the United States.

Section 4. The President, Vice President and all civil Officers of the United States, shall be removed from Office on Impeachment for, and Conviction of, Treason, Bribery, or other High Crimes and Misdemeanors.

ARTICLE III

Section 1. The judicial Power of the United States, shall be vested in one supreme Court, and in such inferior Courts as the Congress may from time to time ordain and establish. The Judges, both of the supreme and inferior Courts, shall hold their Offices during good Behaviour, and shall, at stated Times, receive for their Services, a Compensation, which shall not be diminished during their Continuance in Office.

Section 2. The judicial Power shall extend to all Cases, in Law and Equity, arising under this Constitution, the Laws of the United States, and Treaties made, or which shall be made, under their Authority;—to all Cases affecting Ambassador, other public Ministers and Consuls;—to all Cases of admiralty and maritime Jurisdiction;—to Controversies to which the United States shall be a Party;—to Controversies between two or more States;—between a State and Citizens of another State; between Citizens of different States;—between Citizens of the same State claiming Lands under Grants of different States, and between a State, or the Citizens thereof, and foreign States, Citizens or Subjects.

In all Cases affecting Ambassadors, other public Ministers and Consuls, and those in which a State shall be Party, the supreme Court shall have original Jurisdiction. In all the other cases before mentioned, the supreme Court shall have appellate Jurisdiction, both as to Law and Fact, with such Exceptions, and under such Regulations as the Congress shall make.

The Trial of all Crimes, except in Cases of Impeachment, shall be by Jury; and such Trial shall be held in the State where the said Crimes shall have been committed; but when not committed within any State, the Trial shall be at such Place or Places as the Congress may by Law have directed.

Section 3. Treason against the United States, shall consist only in levying War against them, or in adhering to their Enemies, giving them Aid and Comfort. No person shall be convicted of Treason unless on the Testimony of two Witnesses to the same overt Act, or on Confession in open Court.

The Congress shall have power to declare the Punishment of Treason but no Attainder of Treason shall work Corruption of Blood, or Forfeiture except during the Life of the Person attainted.

ARTICLE IV

Section 1. Full Faith and Credit shall be given in each State to the public Act, Records, and judicial Proceedings of every other State. And the Congress may by general Laws prescribe the Manner in which such Acts, Records and Proceedings shall be proved, and the Effect thereof.

Section 2. The Citizens of each State shall be entitled to all Privileges and Immunities of Citizens in the several States.

A Person charged in any State with Treason, Felony, or other Crime, who shall flee from Justice, and be found in another State, shall on Demand of the executive Authority of the State from which he fled, be delivered up, to be removed to the State having Jurisdiction of the Crime.

No Person held to Service or Labour in one State, under the Laws thereof, escaping into another, shall, in Con-

sequence of any Law or Regulation therein, be discharged
from such Service or Labour, but shall be delivered up on
Claim of the Party to whom such Service or Labour may
be due.

Section 3. New States may be admitted by the Congress into this Union; but no new State shall be formed or
erected within the Jurisdiction of any other State; nor any
State be formed by the Junction of two or more States, or
Parts of States, without the Consent of the Legislatures of
the States concerned as well as of the Congress.

The Congress shall have Power to dispose of and make
all needful Rules and Regulations respecting the Territory
or other Property belonging to the United States; and
nothing in this Constitution shall be so construed as to
Prejudice any Claims of the United States, or of any particular State.

Section 4. The United States shall guarantee to every
State in this Union a Republican Form of Government,
and shall protect each of them against Invasion; and on
Application of the Legislature, or of the Executive (when
the Legislature cannot be convened) against domestic Violence.

Article V

The Congress, whenever two thirds of both Houses
shall deem it necessary, shall propose Amendments to this
Constitution, or, on the Application of the Legislatures of
two thirds of the several States, shall call a Convention for
proposing Amendments, which, in either Case, shall be
valid to all Intents and Purposes, as Part of this Constitution, when ratified by the Legislatures of three fourths of
the several States, or by Conventions in three fourths
thereof, as the one or the other Mode of Ratification may
be proposed by the Congress; Provided that no Amendment which may be made prior to the Year one thousand

eight hundred and eight shall in any Manner affect the first and fourth Clauses in the Ninth Section of the first Article; and that no State, without its Consent, shall be deprived of its equal Suffrage in the Senate.

ARTICLE VI

All Debts contracted and Engagements entered into, before the Adoption of this Constitution, shall be as valid against the United States under this Constitution, as under the Confederation.

This Constitution, and the Laws of the United States which shall be made in Pursuance thereof; and all Treaties made, or which shall be made, under the Authority of the United States, shall be the supreme Law of the Land; and the Judges in every State shall be bound thereby, any Thing in the Constitution or Laws of any State to the Contrary notwithstanding.

The Senators and Representatives before mentioned, and the Members of the several State Legislatures, and all executive and judicial Officers, both of the United States and of the several States, shall be bound by Oath or Affirmation, to support this Constitution; but no religious Test shall ever be required as a Qualification to any Office or public Trust under the United States.

ARTICLE VII

The Ratification of the Conventions of nine States, shall be sufficient for the Establishment of this Constitution between the States so ratifying the Same.

DONE in Convention by the Unanimous Consent of the States present the Seventeenth Day of September in the Year of our Lord one thousand seven hundred and eighty seven and of the Independence of the United States of America the Twelfth.

IN WITNESS whereof We have hereunto subscribed our Names,

GEORGE WASHINGTON—President
and deputy from Virginia

AMENDMENTS

First 10 Amendments adopted December 15, 1791— "Bill of Rights."

Amendment 1

Congress shall make no law respecting an establishment of religion, or prohibiting the free exercise thereof; or abridging the freedom of speech, or of the press; or the right of the people peaceably to assemble, and to petition the Government for a redress of grievances.

Amendment 2

A well regulated Militia, being necessary to the security of a free State, the right of the people to keep and bear arms, shall not be infringed.

Amendment 3

No soldier shall, in time of peace be quartered in any house, without the consent of the owner, nor in time of war, but in a manner to be prescribed by law.

Amendment 4

The right of the people to be secure in their persons, houses, papers, and effects, against unreasonable searches and seizures, shall not be violated, and no warrants shall issue, but upon probable cause, supported by oath or affirmation, and particularly describing the place to be searched, and the persons or things to be seized.

Amendment 5

No person shall be held to answer for a capital, or otherwise infamous crime, unless on a presentment or indictment of a Grand Jury, except in cases arising in the land or naval forces, or in the Militia, when in actual service in time of war or public danger; nor shall any person be subject for the same offense to be twice put in jeopardy of life or limb; nor shall be compelled in any criminal case to be a witness against himself, nor be deprived of life, liberty, or property, without due process of law; nor shall private property be taken for public use, without just compensation.

Amendment 6

In all criminal prosecutions, the accused shall enjoy the right to a speedy and public trial, by an impartial jury of the State and district wherein the crime shall have been committed, which district shall have been previously ascertained by law, and to be informed of the nature and cause of the accusation; to be confronted with the witnesses against him; to have compulsory process for obtaining witnesses in his favor, and to have the assistance of counsel for his defence.

Amendment 7

In suits at common law, where the value in controversy shall exceed twenty dollars, the right of trial by jury shall be preserved, and no fact tried by a jury, shall be otherwise re-examined in any court of the United States, than according to the rules of the common law.

Amendment 8

Excessive bail shall not be required, no excessive fines imposed, nor cruel and unusual punishments inflicted.

Amendment 9

The enumeration in the Constitution, of certain rights, shall not be construed to deny or disparage others retained by the people.

Amendment 10

The powers not delegated to the United States by the Constitution, nor prohibited by it to the States, are reserved to the States respectively, or to the people.

Amendment 11—(*Adopted January 8, 1798*)

The judicial power of the United States shall not be construed to extend to any suit in law or equity, commenced or prosecuted against one of the United States by citizens of another State, or by citizens or subjects of any foreign State.

Amendment 12—(*Adopted September 25, 1804*)

The electors shall meet in their respective states and vote by ballot for President and Vice-President, one of whom, at least, shall not be an inhabitant of the same state with themselves; they shall name in their ballots the person voted for as President, and in distinct ballots the persons voted for as Vice-President, and they shall make distinct lists of all persons voted for as President, and of all persons voted for as Vice-President, and of the number of votes for each, which lists they shall sign and certify, and transmit sealed to the seat of the government of the United States, directed to the President of the Senate;— The President of the Senate shall, in the presence of the Senate and House of Representatives, open all the certificates and the votes shall then be counted;—the person having the greatest number of votes for President, shall be the President, if such number be a majority of the whole number of electors appointed; and if no person have such majority, then from the persons having the highest numbers not exceeding three on the list of those voted for as President, the House of Representatives shall choose immediately, by ballot, the President. But in choosing the President, the votes shall be taken by states, the representation from each state having one vote; a quorum for this purpose shall consist of a member or members from two-thirds of the states, and a majority of all the states shall be necessary to a choice. And if the House of Representatives shall not choose a President whenever the right of choice shall devolve upon them, before the fourth day of March next following, then the Vice-President shall act as President, as in the case of the death or other constitutional disability of the President.—The person having the greatest number of votes as Vice-President, shall be the Vice-President, if such number be a majority of the whole number of electors appointed, and if no person have a majority, then from the two highest numbers on the list, the Senate shall choose the Vice-President; a quorum for the purpose shall consist of two-thirds of the whole number of Senators, and a majority of the whole number shall be necessary to a choice. But no person constitutionally ineligible to the office of President shall be eligible to that of Vice-President of the United States.

Amendment 13—(Adopted December 18, 1865)

Section 1. Neither slavery nor involuntary servitude, except as a punishment for crime whereof the party shall have been duly convicted, shall exist within the United States, or any place subject to their jurisdiction.

Section 2. Congress shall have power to enforce this article by appropriate legislation.

Amendment 14—(Adopted July 28, 1868)

Section 1. All persons born or naturalized in the United States, and subject to the jurisdiction thereof, are citizens of the United States and of the State wherein they reside. No State shall make or enforce any law which shall abridge the privileges or immunities of citizens of 'the United States; nor shall any State deprive any person of life, liberty, or property, without due process of law; nor deny to any person within its jurisdiction the equal protection of the laws.

Section 2. Representatives shall be apportioned among the several States according to their respective numbers, counting the whole number of persons in each State, excluding Indians not taxed. But when the right to vote at any election for the choice of electors for President and Vice President of the United States, Representatives in Congress, the executive and judicial officers of a State, or the members of the Legislature thereof, is denied to any of the male inhabitants of such State, being twenty-one years of age, and citizens of the United States, or in any way abridged, except for participation in rebellion, or other crime, the basis of representation therein shall be reduced in the proportion which the number of such male citizens shall bear to the whole number of male citizens twenty-one years of age in such State.

Section 3. No person shall be a Senator or Representative in Congress, or elector of President and Vice President, or hold any office, civil or military, under the United States, or under any State, who, having previously taken an oath, as a member of Congress, or as an officer of the United States, or as a member of any State legislature, or as an executive or judicial officer of any State, to support the Constitution of the United States, shall have engaged in insurrection or rebellion against the same, or given aid or comfort to the enemies thereof. But Congress may by a vote of two-thirds of each House, remove such disability.

Section 4. The validity of the public debt of the United States, authorized by law, including debts incurred for payment of pensions and bounties for services in suppressing insurrection or rebellion, shall not be questioned. But neither the United States nor any State shall assume or pay any debt or obligation incurred in aid of insurrection or rebellion against the United States, or any claim for the loss or emancipation of any slave; but all such debts, obligations and claims shall be held illegal and void.

Section 5. The Congress shall have power to enforce, by appropriate legislation, the provisions of this article.

Amendment 15—(*Adopted March 30, 1870*)

Section 1. The right of citizens of the United States to vote shall not be denied or abridged by the United States or by any State on account of race, color, or previous condition of servitude.

Section 2. The Congress shall have power to enforce this article by appropriate legislation.

Amendment 16—(*Adopted February 25, 1913*)

The Congress shall have power to lay and collect taxes on incomes, from whatever source derived, without apportionment among the several States, and without regard to any census or enumeration.

Amendment 17—(*Adopted May 31, 1913*)

The Senate of the United States shall be composed of two Senators from each State elected by the people thereof for six years; and each Senator shall have one vote. The electors in each State shall have the qualifications requisite for electors of the most numerous branch of the State legislatures.

When vacancies happen in the representation of any State in the Senate, the executive authority of such State shall issue writs of election to fill such vacancies: *Provided,* That the legislature of any State may empower the executive thereof to make temporary appointments until the people fill the vacancies by election as the legislature may direct.

This amendment shall not be so construed as to affect the election or term of any Senator chosen before it becomes valid as part of the Constitution.

Amendment 18—(*Adopted January 29, 1919*)

Section 1. After one year from the ratification of this article the manufacture, sale, or transportation of intoxicating liquors within, the importation thereof into, or the exportation thereof from the United States and all territory subject to the jurisdiction thereof for beverage purposes is hereby prohibited.

Section 2. The Congress and the several States shall have concurrent power to enforce this article by appropriate legislation.

Amendment 19—(*Adopted August 26, 1920*)

The right of citizens of the United States to vote shall not be denied or abridged by the United States or by any State on account of sex.

Congress shall have power to enforce this article by appropriate legislation.

Amendment 20—(*Adopted February 6, 1933*)

Section 1. The terms of the President and Vice President shall end at noon on the 20th day of January, and the terms of Senators and Representatives at noon on the 3d day of January, of the years in which such terms would have ended if this article had not been ratified; and the terms of their successors shall then begin.

Section 2. The Congress shall assemble at least once in every year, and such meeting shall begin at noon on the 3d day of January, unless they shall by law appoint a different day.

Section 3. If, at the time fixed for the beginning of the term of the President, the President elect shall have died, the Vice President elect shall become President. If a President shall not have been chosen before the time fixed for the beginning of his term, or if the President elect shall have failed to qualify, then the Vice President elect shall act as President until a President shall have qualified; and the Congress may by law provide for the case wherein neither a President elect nor a Vice President elect shall have qualified, declaring who shall then act as President, or the manner in which one who is to act shall be selected, and such person shall act accordingly until a President or Vice President shall have qualified.

Section 4. The Congress may by law provide for the case of the death of any of the persons from whom the House of Representatives may choose a President whenever the right of choice shall have devolved upon them, and for the case of the death of any of the persons from whom the Senate may choose a Vice President whenever the right of choice shall have devolved upon them.

Section 5. Sections 1 and 2 shall take effect on the 15th day of October following the ratification of this article.

Amendment 21—(*Adopted December 5, 1933*)

Section 1. The eighteenth article of amendment to the Constitution of the United States is hereby repealed.

Amendment 22—(*Adopted February 26, 1951*)

No person shall be elected to office of the President more than twice, and no person who has held the office of President, or acted as President, for more than two years of a term to which some other person was elected President shall be elected to the office of the President more than once. But this Article shall not apply to any person holding the office of President when this Article was proposed by the Congress, and shall not prevent any person who may be holding the office of President, or acting as President, during the term within which this Article becomes operative from holding the office of President or acting as President during the remainder of such term.

INDEX